Copyright © 2024 Charles Mackey

All rights reserved

The characters and events portrayed in this book are fictitious. Any similarity to real persons, living or dead, is coincidental and not intended by the author.

No part of this book may be reproduced, or stored in a retrieval system, or transmitted in any form or by any means, electronic, mechanical, photocopying, recording, or otherwise, without express written permission of the publisher.

ISBN- 9798346016175

Cover design by: C. L. Mackery
Library of Congress Control Number: 2018675309
Printed in the United States of America

I would like to dedicate this book to my Father Lorenzo Mackey and my older brother Jay Mackey. They're the men that lead me to God. Thank you.

CONTENTS

Copyright
Dedication
Introduction
Chapter 1: Integrity and Honesty in Business   2
Chapter 2: Stewardship and Responsibility   11
Chapter 3: Leadership Lessons from Biblical Figures   21
Chapter 4: King Solomon's Business Model   30
Chapter 5: The Model of Servant Leadership   44
Chapter 6: Wealth, Money, and Ethical Profit   57
Chapter 7: Justice and Fairness in the Marketplace   72
Chapter 8: The Importance of Vision and Planning   84
Chapter 9: Cultivating a Strong Work Ethic   99
Chapter 10: Navigating Competition and Conflict   111
Chapter 11: The Principle of Rest and Renewal   129
Chapter 12:Conclusion: Building a Business That Lasts   142
Chapter 13: Final Thoughts   147

INTRODUCTION

Introduction

In an era defined by rapid technological advancements and shifting economic landscapes, businesses are constantly seeking foundational principles that transcend fleeting trends. While innovative strategies and contemporary theories offer valuable insights, there exists a reservoir of ancient wisdom that has guided individuals and societies for millennia—the Bible.

"Faith & Fortune: A biblical guide to business" is a journey into the timeless teachings of the Bible and their profound relevance to today's business world. This book is not about religion per se; it's about exploring universal principles embedded in biblical texts that can inform ethical decision-making, leadership styles, and sustainable business practices.

The Bible offers more than spiritual guidance; it provides practical lessons on integrity, stewardship, leadership, and the responsible management of resources. From the wisdom of King Solomon—whose reign epitomized prosperity and astute governance—to the parables of Jesus that underscore the value of servant leadership and ethical conduct, these ancient narratives hold invaluable lessons for modern entrepreneurs, executives, and professionals alike.

In these pages, you will discover:

- **Timeless Principles of Integrity and Honesty**: Learn how transparent and ethical practices build lasting trust with stakeholders and lay the foundation for enduring success.
- **Insights into Effective Leadership**: Draw inspiration from biblical figures who demonstrated exceptional leadership qualities, and understand how to apply these lessons in guiding teams and organizations today.
- **The Art of Wise Stewardship**: Explore the importance of managing not just financial assets but also human and environmental resources responsibly.
- **Strategies for Sustainable Growth**: Delve into King Solomon's business model, examining his approaches to administration, international trade, and wealth accumulation, and how these can be adapted to the contemporary business environment.
- **The Power of Servant Leadership**: Understand how prioritizing the needs of others can transform organizational culture and drive performance.
- **Balancing Wealth and Ethics**: Reflect on the pursuit of profit in light of ethical considerations, ensuring that financial success does not come at the expense of moral integrity.

This book also addresses practical challenges such as navigating competition, resolving conflicts, and preventing burnout through the principle of rest and renewal. Each chapter is designed to bridge the gap between ancient wisdom and modern application, providing actionable insights backed by scriptural references.

Whether you are a seasoned executive, a budding entrepreneur, or someone interested in the intersection of faith and business, this book offers a comprehensive guide to building a business that is not only profitable but also principled and purpose-driven.

In embracing these biblical principles, we find that successful business practices and ethical integrity are not mutually exclusive but are, in fact, deeply interconnected. By aligning our professional endeavors with these timeless teachings, we can contribute to a more just, sustainable, and prosperous society.

Join us on this enlightening journey as we uncover the enduring wisdom of the Bible and its transformative impact on modern commerce.

CHARLES L MACKEY

CHAPTER 1: INTEGRITY AND HONESTY IN BUSINESS

"Dishonest scales are an abomination to the LORD, but a just weight is His delight." — *Proverbs 11:1

Introduction

Integrity and honesty are the cornerstones of a successful and sustainable business. In an era where cutting corners and ethical compromises might yield short-term gains, the Bible emphasizes the enduring value of honesty. This chapter delves into how transparent dealings not only build trust with customers and partners but also align businesses with a higher ethical standard that fosters long-term success.

The Cost of Dishonesty in Business Relationships

Erosion Of Trust

Trust is fundamental in any business relationship. Dishonesty, whether through misleading marketing, hidden fees, or subpar product quality, undermines this trust.

- *Customer Loss*: Customers who feel deceived are unlikely to return and may dissuade others through negative reviews and word-of-mouth.
- **Employee Morale**: Employees may become disengaged if they perceive unethical practices, leading to decreased productivity and higher turnover.
- **Partnership Strains**: Business partners may sever ties if they cannot rely on your integrity.

Legal And Financial Repercussions

- **Regulatory Fines**: Governments enforce laws against fraudulent practices. Violations can result in hefty fines and sanctions.
- **Lawsuits**: Dishonesty can lead to lawsuits from customers, employees, or competitors, resulting in legal fees and potential settlements.
- **Loss of Licenses**: Persistent unethical behavior may lead to revocation of business licenses or certifications.

Reputation Damage

In today's digital age, news about dishonest practices spreads rapidly.

- **Negative Publicity**: Scandals can attract media attention, damaging your brand image.
- **Investor Confidence**: Investors may withdraw support if they perceive ethical risks, affecting capital and stock prices.

Biblical Insight

- *"Bread gained by deceit is sweet to a man, but afterward his mouth will be filled with gravel."* — *Proverbs 20:17*

This proverb warns that while dishonesty might offer immediate gratification, it ultimately leads to regret and dissatisfaction.

Building Brand Reputation Through Integrity

Trust As A Competitive Advantage

- **Companies known for integrity often enjoy:**
- **Customer Loyalty**: Trustworthy businesses cultivate loyal customers who may pay premium prices and act as brand ambassadors.
- **Employee Retention**: Ethical workplaces attract and retain top talent who value integrity.
- **Strong Partnerships**: Other businesses prefer to partner

with companies they can trust.

Creating A Culture Of Integrity

- **Leadership Example**: Leaders must embody the ethical standards they wish to see, as their actions set the tone for the organization.
- **Transparent Communication**: Openness about company policies, pricing, and operations builds trust with stakeholders.
- **Consistent Policies**: Applying rules and procedures fairly to all employees reinforces a culture of honesty.

Implementing Ethical Policies

- **Code of Ethics**: Develop a clear code that outlines expected behaviors and consequences for violations.
- **Ethics Training**: Regular training helps employees navigate ethical dilemmas and reinforces the importance of integrity.
- **Accountability Systems**: Establish checks and balances to prevent and detect unethical behavior.

Biblical Insight

- **"Better is a poor person who walks in his integrity than one who is crooked in speech and is a fool."** — *Proverbs 19:1*

This verse highlights that integrity is more valuable than wealth gained through dishonest means.

*Case Studies of Companies
That Prioritize Honesty*

Case Study 1: Patagonia

- **Environmental Commitment**: Patagonia donates a portion of its profits to environmental causes and is transparent about its supply chain.
- **Customer Trust**: Their honesty about product impact builds credibility, fostering a loyal customer base.
- **Business Success**: Despite higher prices, customers support Patagonia for its integrity, leading to sustained profitability.

Case Study 2: The Johnson & Johnson Tylenol Crisis

- **Proactive Measures**: In 1982, after tampering incidents, Johnson & Johnson recalled all Tylenol products, prioritizing consumer safety over profit.
- **Transparent Communication**: They kept the public informed throughout the crisis.
- **Rebuilding Trust**: Their honest approach restored consumer confidence and set industry standards for crisis management.

Case Study 3: Whole Foods Market

- **Transparency**: Whole Foods shares information about product sourcing, pricing, and store operations.
- **Employee Engagement**: They foster an open culture where employees are encouraged to voice concerns.
- **Customer Loyalty**: Shoppers appreciate the honesty, contributing to the company's strong market position.

Biblical Insight

- *"Whoever walks in integrity walks securely, but he who makes his ways crooked will be found out."* — *Proverbs 10:9*

Integrity leads to security and stability, while dishonesty eventually leads to exposure and downfall.

Practical Steps to Foster Integrity in Business

Establish Clear Core Values

- **Define Values**: Clearly articulate what integrity means for your organization.
- **Communicate**: Ensure all employees understand and embrace these values.

Lead By Example

- **Model Behavior**: Leaders should demonstrate integrity in all actions, setting the standard for others.
- **Mentorship**: Guide employees on ethical decision-making.

Implement Accountability Measures

- **Whistleblower Policies**: Encourage reporting of unethical behavior without fear of retaliation.
- **Regular Audits**: Conduct internal audits to ensure compliance with ethical standards.

Promote Transparency

- **Open Communication**: Share both successes and failures openly with stakeholders.
- **Accessible Information**: Make company policies and procedures easily accessible to all employees.

Invest In Ethics Training

- **Workshops and Seminars**: Provide regular training on

ethical issues relevant to your industry.
- **Scenario Planning**: Use real-life scenarios to help employees practice ethical decision-making.

Conclusion

Embracing integrity and honesty is not just about adhering to moral obligations; it's a strategic approach that builds a solid foundation for long-term success. Businesses that prioritize these values create trust, foster loyalty, and differentiate themselves in competitive markets. The biblical teachings provide timeless wisdom, reminding us that integrity delights the Lord and leads to security and prosperity.

Reflection Questions

1. **Self-Assessment**: In what areas does your business excel in integrity, and where is there room for improvement?
2. **Action Plan**: What specific steps can you take to enhance transparency and honesty in your organization?
3. **Leadership Role**: How can you, as a leader, model integrity in your daily actions and decisions?

Key Scriptures for Further Reflection

- **Proverbs 11:1**: On honest dealings.
- **Proverbs 20:17**: The fleeting satisfaction of deceit.
- **Proverbs 19:1**: Valuing integrity over dishonest gain.
- **Proverbs 10:9**: The security that comes with integrity.

End of Chapter 1

CHAPTER 2: STEWARDSHIP AND RESPONSIBILITY

"For the kingdom of heaven is like a man traveling to a far country, who called his own servants and delivered his goods to them." — *Matthew 25:14*

Introduction

Stewardship is a fundamental concept that transcends time and culture, emphasizing the responsible management of resources entrusted to us. In the Parable of the Talents (*Matthew 25:14-30*), Jesus illustrates the importance of utilizing our gifts and resources effectively. This chapter explores how businesses can embrace stewardship by wisely managing financial capital, human talent, and environmental resources to achieve growth and make a positive impact on society.

Maximizing Resources for Growth and Impact

Understanding The Parable Of The Talents

In the parable, a master entrusts his servants with varying amounts of money (talents) before embarking on a journey. Upon his return, he assesses how each servant managed the resources:

- **Faithful Servants**: Those who invested and doubled their talents were commended and rewarded.
- **Unfaithful Servant**: The one who hid his talent out of fear was reprimanded and faced consequences.

Application To Business

- **Resource Allocation**: Businesses are entrusted with resources—capital, personnel, time—that must be managed wisely.
- **Investment in Growth**: Like the faithful servants, companies should invest resources to generate returns, fostering innovation and expansion.
- **Risk Management**: Avoiding action out of fear, like the unfaithful servant, can hinder progress. Calculated risks are essential for growth.

Strategies for Maximizing Resources

1. **Assessing Assets and Opportunities**

    - **Inventory of Resources**: Regularly evaluate financial assets, intellectual property, and human capital.

- **Market Analysis**: Identify opportunities for expansion or diversification that align with core competencies.

2. **Employee Development**

   - **Training Programs**: Invest in employee education to enhance skills and productivity.
   - **Empowerment**: Encourage employees to take initiative and contribute ideas.

3. **Innovation and Adaptation**

   - **Research and Development**: Allocate funds for innovation to stay competitive.
   - **Embracing Technology**: Utilize technological advancements to improve efficiency.

Biblical Insight

- **"Moreover, it is required in stewards that one be found faithful."** — *1 Corinthians 4:2*

Faithfulness in stewardship is demonstrated through diligent and effective management of what has been entrusted.

Corporate Social Responsibility as Modern Stewardship

Defining Corporate Social Responsibility (Csr)

CSR refers to a company's commitment to operate ethically and contribute to economic development while improving the quality of life for employees, the community, and society at large.

The Link Between Stewardship And Csr

- **Ethical Obligation**: Stewardship extends beyond profit, encompassing ethical responsibilities toward stakeholders.
- **Societal Impact**: Businesses have the power to effect positive change through sustainable practices and community engagement.

Implementing Csr Initiatives

1. **Community Engagement**

    - **Philanthropy**: Support charitable causes through donations and sponsorships.
    - **Volunteer Programs**: Encourage employee participation in community service.

2. **Ethical Business Practices**

    - **Fair Labor Policies**: Ensure safe working conditions and fair compensation.
    - **Transparent Governance**: Maintain honesty and integrity

in all operations.

3. **Environmental Responsibility**

   - **Sustainable Sourcing**: Use materials and suppliers that adhere to environmental standards.
   - **Carbon Footprint Reduction**: Implement energy-efficient processes and reduce waste.

Benefits Of Csr

- **Enhanced Reputation**: Companies known for social responsibility attract customers and talent.
- **Customer Loyalty**: Consumers increasingly prefer brands that align with their values.
- **Long-Term Profitability**: Ethical practices can lead to sustainable financial performance.

Biblical Insight

- **"As each has received a gift, use it to serve one another, as good stewards of God's varied grace."** — *1 Peter 4:10*

   This verse emphasizes using our gifts to serve others, reflecting the essence of CSR.

Sustainable Practices in

Business Operations

The Importance Of Environmental Stewardship

Stewardship involves caring for the Earth, recognizing that natural resources are finite and must be preserved for future generations.

Integrating Sustainability

1. **Resource Efficiency**

   - **Energy Conservation**: Utilize renewable energy sources and optimize energy use.
   - **Water Management**: Implement systems to reduce water consumption and waste.

2. **Waste Reduction**

   - **Recycling Programs**: Encourage recycling within the company and with consumers.
   - **Product Lifecycle Management**: Design products with end-of-life recycling in mind.

3. **Sustainable Supply Chains**

   - **Ethical Sourcing**: Partner with suppliers committed to sustainable practices.
   - **Local Procurement**: Source materials locally to reduce transportation emissions.

Case Studies Of Sustainable Businesses

- **Unilever**

  - **Sustainable Living Plan**: Aims to decouple growth from environmental impact.
  - **Social Impact**: Focuses on improving health and well-being for millions.

- **IKEA**

  - **Renewable Energy Commitment**: Invested heavily in wind and solar energy.
  - **Sustainable Materials**: Aims to use only renewable and recycled materials by 2030.

Biblical Insight

- **"The Earth is the Lord's, and everything in it."** — *Psalm 24:1*

   Recognizing that the Earth belongs to God reinforces our responsibility to care for it.

Practical Steps to Embrace Stewardship

Develop A Stewardship Mindset

- **Mission and Vision Alignment**: Integrate stewardship into the company's core values.
- **Leadership Commitment**: Executives must champion stewardship initiatives.

Set Measurable Goals

- **Environmental Targets**: Establish clear objectives for reducing emissions and waste.
- **Social Objectives**: Define goals for community impact and employee welfare.

Engage Stakeholders

- **Employee Involvement**: Foster a culture where employees participate in stewardship efforts.
- **Customer Collaboration**: Educate and involve customers in sustainability initiatives.

Monitor And Report Progress

- **Transparency**: Regularly report on stewardship efforts and outcomes.

- **Continuous Improvement**: Use feedback to enhance strategies and practices.

Conclusion

Stewardship and responsibility are not merely ethical considerations but strategic imperatives in today's business environment. By maximizing resources, embracing corporate social responsibility, and implementing sustainable practices, businesses can achieve growth while contributing positively to society and the environment. The biblical principles of stewardship remind us that we are caretakers of the resources entrusted to us, called to use them wisely for the greater good.

Reflection Questions

1. **Resource Management**: How effectively is your organization utilizing its resources? Where can improvements be made?
2. **CSR Engagement**: In what ways can your company enhance its commitment to social responsibility?
3. **Sustainability Practices**: What steps can you take to make your operations more environmentally sustainable?

Key Scriptures for Further Reflection

- **Matthew 25:14-30**: The Parable of the Talents.
- **1 Corinthians 4:2**: Faithfulness in stewardship.

- **1 Peter 4:10**: Using gifts to serve others.
- **Psalm 24:1**: The Earth belongs to the Lord.

End of Chapter 2

CHAPTER 3: LEADERSHIP LESSONS FROM BIBLICAL FIGURES

"Where there is no counsel, the people fall; but in the multitude of counselors there is safety." — *Proverbs 11:14*

Introduction

Leadership is a critical element in the success of any organization. The Bible offers rich narratives of leaders who demonstrated exceptional qualities, providing timeless lessons that can be applied in today's business environment. Figures like Moses, who led with patience, and Nehemiah, who rebuilt against opposition, exemplify leadership marked by vision, resilience, humility, and service. This chapter explores their experiences and extracts principles that can inform contemporary leadership styles.

The Role of Vision in Leadership

Moses: Leading With A Clear Vision

Moses is one of the most prominent leaders in the Bible. Tasked with leading the Israelites out of Egyptian bondage, he exemplified the importance of having a clear vision.

- **Defining the Vision**: Moses communicated God's promise of freedom and a land flowing with milk and honey, providing a clear destination for his people.
- **Communicating the Vision**: He regularly conveyed the vision to the Israelites, reminding them of their purpose and encouraging them during challenging times.
- **Staying Committed to the Vision**: Despite setbacks and opposition, Moses remained steadfast, demonstrating the necessity of perseverance.

Application To Business

- **Establishing a Compelling Vision**: Leaders should define clear, inspiring goals that align with the organization's mission.
- **Effective Communication**: Regularly sharing the vision with the team ensures alignment and motivates employees.
- **Perseverance**: Commitment to the vision helps navigate obstacles and maintain focus during difficult periods.

Nehemiah: Vision For Rebuilding

Nehemiah, upon hearing about the ruined walls of Jerusalem, was moved to action.

- **Assessing the Situation**: Nehemiah took the time to understand the extent of the damage.
- **Strategic Planning**: He developed a plan to rebuild the walls, assigning specific tasks to different groups.
- **Inspiring Others**: Nehemiah motivated the people by sharing his vision of a restored Jerusalem.

Application To Business

- **Situation Analysis**: Leaders should assess their organization's current state before implementing changes.
- **Strategic Planning**: Developing a detailed plan with assigned responsibilities enhances efficiency.
- **Inspiration**: Sharing a hopeful vision can galvanize a team to achieve collective goals.

Biblical Insight

- **"Write the vision and make it plain on tablets, that he may run who reads it."** — *Habakkuk 2:2*

Clarity in vision enables swift and focused action.

Overcoming Adversity and Opposition

Moses: Facing Challenges

-**Moses encountered numerous challenges:**
- **Resistance from Pharaoh**: Persistently demanded the release of the Israelites despite repeated refusals.
- **Doubt Among the People**: Faced complaints and lack of faith from the Israelites.
- **Logistical Challenges**: Led a large population through the desert with limited resources.

Strategies Employed

- **Faith and Courage**: Moses relied on his faith to confront powerful opposition.
- **Problem-Solving**: Addressed practical needs, such as providing food and water.
- **Intercession**: Acted as an intermediary between God and the people, seeking guidance.

Nehemiah: Overcoming Opposition

Nehemiah faced external and internal opposition:

- **Enemies Mocking and Threatening**: Sanballat and Tobiah ridiculed and plotted against the rebuilding efforts.
- **Internal Strife**: Economic hardships among the workers led to discontent.

Strategies Employed

- **Prayer and Vigilance**: Combined spiritual reliance with practical measures, like setting guards.
- **Addressing Internal Issues**: Resolved economic injustices by urging nobles to forgive debts.

Application To Business

- **Anticipating Opposition**: Leaders should expect challenges and prepare accordingly.
- **Resilience**: Maintaining determination in the face of adversity is crucial.
- **Conflict Resolution**: Addressing internal issues promptly prevents them from derailing progress.

Biblical Insight

- **"Consider it pure joy... whenever you face trials of many kinds, because you know that the testing of your faith produces perseverance."** — *James 1:2-3*

  Adversity develops strength and character.

Leading with Humility and Service

Moses: A Humble Leader

- **Reluctant Leadership**: Initially hesitant to lead, acknowledging his own limitations.
- **Servant Attitude**: Prioritized the needs of the people over his own comfort.
- **Intercessory Prayer**: Often pleaded on behalf of the Israelites, even when they erred.

Nehemiah: Servant Leadership

- **Personal Sacrifice**: Refused the governor's provisions to lighten the burden on the people.
- **Hands-On Approach**: Worked alongside the builders, demonstrating commitment.

Application To Business

- **Humility**: Recognizing one's limitations fosters a collaborative environment.
- **Empathy**: Understanding and addressing the needs of employees builds trust.
- **Lead by Example**: Participating in the work inspires others and demonstrates solidarity.

Biblical Insight

- *"But among you it will be different. Whoever wants to be a leader among you must be your servant."** — *Matthew 20:26*

True leadership is characterized by service to others.

Practical Steps for Contemporary Leaders

Develop A Clear Vision

- **Define Objectives**: Articulate clear, achievable goals.
- **Engage Stakeholders**: Involve team members in the vision-crafting process.
- **Communicate Regularly**: Keep the vision at the forefront through consistent messaging.

Build Resilience

- **Prepare for Challenges**: Anticipate potential obstacles and plan responses.
- **Cultivate a Positive Mindset**: Encourage optimism and perseverance within the team.
- **Learn from Setbacks**: View failures as learning opportunities.

Embrace Servant Leadership

- **Prioritize Team Needs**: Focus on supporting employees to

achieve their best.
- **Demonstrate Humility**: Admit mistakes and be open to feedback.
- **Lead by Example**: Model the behavior and work ethic expected from others.

Conclusion

The leadership lessons from Moses and Nehemiah offer valuable insights for modern business leaders. By embodying a clear vision, demonstrating resilience in the face of adversity, and leading with humility and service, leaders can inspire their teams to achieve extraordinary results. The biblical narratives reinforce that effective leadership is not about wielding power but about guiding others towards a common goal with wisdom and compassion.

Reflection Questions

1. **Vision Clarity**: Is your organization's vision clearly defined and communicated to all team members?
2. **Adversity Management**: How do you currently handle opposition or challenges? What can you learn from Moses and Nehemiah's approaches?
3. **Servant Leadership**: In what ways can you incorporate humility and service into your leadership style?

Key Scriptures for Further Reflection

- **Proverbs 11:14**: The importance of wise counsel.
- **Habakkuk 2:2**: Writing and communicating the vision.
- **James 1:2-3**: Perseverance through trials.
- **Matthew 20:26**: The call to servant leadership.

End of Chapter 3

CHAPTER 4: KING SOLOMON'S BUSINESS MODEL

"So King Solomon surpassed all the kings of the earth in riches and wisdom." — *1 Kings 10:23*

Introduction

King Solomon is renowned not only for his unparalleled wisdom but also for his immense wealth and successful governance. His reign is a prime example of how wisdom, strategic planning, and effective leadership can lead to prosperity and influence. This chapter delves deep into Solomon's approach to leadership, wealth accumulation, trade, and governance, as detailed in *1 Kings 3, 4,* and *10*, as well as *2 Chronicles 10*. By extracting principles from Solomon's reign, we can uncover valuable lessons applicable to modern business practices.

The Value of Wisdom in Leadership and Decision-Making

Solomon's Request For Wisdom

Upon ascending the throne, Solomon faced the daunting task of ruling a vast kingdom. Recognizing his own limitations, he sought divine assistance:

"Therefore give to Your servant an understanding heart to judge Your people, that I may discern between good and evil." — *1 Kings 3:9*

God was pleased with Solomon's request, granting him unparalleled wisdom, and additionally, wealth and honor:

"Behold, I have done according to your words; see, I have given you a wise and understanding heart... And I have also given you what you have not asked: both riches and honor..." — *1 Kings 3:12-13*

Application to Business

Prioritizing Wisdom Over Wealth

- **Seeking Knowledge**: Just as Solomon prioritized wisdom, modern business leaders should value knowledge and continuous learning over immediate financial gains.
- **Informed Decision-Making**: Wisdom enables leaders to make sound judgments, anticipate challenges, and devise

effective strategies.
   - **Ethical Leadership**: Wisdom fosters a sense of justice and morality, guiding leaders to act ethically.

Implementing Wisdom In Business Practices

- **Invest in Personal Development**: Encourage ongoing education and professional development for yourself and your team.
- **Cultivate Critical Thinking**: Promote a culture that values analysis, reflection, and thoughtful decision-making.
- **Seek Diverse Perspectives**: Embrace counsel from advisors and experts to enhance understanding and insight.

Biblical Insight

- *"Wisdom is the principal thing; therefore get wisdom. And in all your getting, get understanding."* — *Proverbs 4:7*

Strategic Organization and Delegation

Administrative Excellence

Solomon's reign was marked by efficient administration and effective delegation:

"And Solomon had twelve governors over all Israel, who provided food for the king and his household; each one made provision for one month of the year." — *1 Kings 4:7*

This system ensured that the kingdom's needs were met consistently without overburdening any single region.

Key Elements Of Solomon's Administration

- **Decentralization**: Dividing responsibilities among governors allowed for efficient management of resources.
- **Accountability**: Each governor was responsible for specific duties, fostering accountability.
- **Specialization**: Officials were appointed based on their abilities, ensuring competence in various areas.

Application To Business

- **Effective Delegation**
  - **Empower Leaders**: Assign responsibilities to competent individuals and trust them to execute tasks.
  - **Clear Roles and Responsibilities**: Define job descriptions and expectations to prevent overlaps and confusion.
  - **Accountability Systems**: Implement performance metrics and regular reviews to ensure objectives are met.

Organizational Structure

  - **Decentralize Operations**: Break down the organization into manageable units or departments.
  - **Promote Specialization**: Encourage employees to develop expertise in specific areas.

Benefits

- **Increased Efficiency**: Streamlined operations lead to better productivity.
- **Scalability**: An effective organizational structure facilitates growth.
- **Employee Development**: Delegation provides opportunities for team members to develop leadership skills.

Biblical Insight

- **"Plans are established by counsel; by wise guidance wage war."** — *Proverbs 20:18*

Building and Maintaining International Relationships

International Trade And Wealth Accumulation

Solomon expanded Israel's influence through strategic trade alliances:

"Also, the ships of Hiram, which brought gold from Ophir, brought great quantities of almug wood and precious stones from Ophir." — *1 Kings 10:11*

The visit from the Queen of Sheba further highlights the international recognition of Solomon's wisdom and wealth:

"Now when the queen of Sheba heard of the fame of Solomon... she came to test him with hard questions." — *1 Kings 10:1*

Key Aspects Of Solomon's Trade

- **Alliances with Neighboring Nations**: Partnerships with kings like Hiram of Tyre facilitated access to valuable resources.
- **Diversification of Imports**: Bringing in gold, precious stones, and exotic goods enriched the kingdom.
- **Cultural Exchange**: Interactions with other nations enhanced knowledge and understanding.

Application to Business

- **Global Partnerships**

- **Identify Strategic Partners**: Collaborate with organizations that complement your business.
    - **Expand into New Markets**: Explore international opportunities to diversify revenue streams.
  - **Cross-Cultural Competence**: Develop an understanding of different cultures to build stronger relationships.

- **Diversification Of Products And Services**

  - **Innovate Offerings**: Introduce new products or services to meet diverse customer needs.
    - **Risk Management**: Diversification can mitigate risks associated with market fluctuations.

Benefits

- **Increased Revenue**: Access to larger markets can boost sales.
- **Competitive Advantage**: Unique partnerships and offerings can differentiate your business.
- **Knowledge Sharing**: International collaborations can lead to new ideas and innovations.

Biblical Insight

- **"Give a portion to seven, or even to eight, for you know not what disaster may happen on earth."** — *Ecclesiastes 11:2*

Learning from the Successes and Failures of Predecessors

Listening To Wise Counsel

After Solomon's death, his son Rehoboam ascended the throne. Faced with a critical decision, he sought advice:

"But he rejected the advice which the elders had given him, and consulted the young men who had grown up with him." — *2 Chronicles 10:8*

Rehoboam's refusal to heed the elders' counsel led to the division of the kingdom.

Lessons From Rehoboam's Mistake

- **Value Experienced Advisors**: The elders had the wisdom and experience to guide the new king effectively.
- **Avoiding Arrogance**: Rehoboam's decision reflected a lack of humility and openness to guidance.
- **Understanding the People's Needs**: He failed to address the concerns of the people, resulting in unrest.

Application to Business

Heeding Experienced Advice

- **Mentorship**: Seek guidance from seasoned professionals who have navigated similar challenges.
- **Inclusive Decision-Making**: Consider diverse perspectives before making significant decisions.
- **Continuous Learning**: Learn from the successes and failures of others to inform your strategies.

- **Generational Leadership Transition**

- **Succession Planning**: Prepare for leadership transitions by training and mentoring successors.
- **Preserving Organizational Culture**: Ensure that core values and principles are upheld during transitions.
- **Adapting to Change**: Balance respect for tradition with the need for innovation.

Biblical Insight

- **"Where there is no guidance, a people falls, but in an abundance of counselors there is safety."** — *Proverbs 11:14*

Balancing Wealth and Wisdom

Solomon's Later Years

Despite his wisdom and wealth, Solomon's later years were marked by certain failures:

"For it was so, when Solomon was old, that his wives turned his heart after other gods... Solomon did evil in the sight of the LORD." — *1 Kings 11:4,6*

Lessons Learned

- **Complacency Risks**: Success can lead to complacency and neglect of foundational principles.
- **Moral Integrity**: Maintaining ethical standards is crucial, regardless of wealth or status.
- **Accountability**: Even the wisest can falter without accountability structures.

Application To Business

  - **Ethical Vigilance**
    - **Regular Self-Assessment**: Periodically evaluate personal and organizational adherence to ethical standards.
    - **Accountability Measures**: Establish checks and balances to prevent misconduct.
      - **Sustainability Focus**: Prioritize long-term integrity over

short-term gains.

Biblical Insight

- **"For what will it profit a man if he gains the whole world, and loses his own soul?"** — *Mark 8:36*

Practical Steps for Implementing Solomon's Principles

1. Seek Wisdom Actively

- **Professional Development**: Invest in education and training programs.
- **Advisory Boards**: Establish a board of advisors with diverse expertise.
- **Mentorship Programs**: Encourage mentorship within the organization.

2. Optimize Organizational Structure

- **Delegation Framework**: Create clear hierarchies and delegation protocols.
- **Talent Development**: Identify and nurture leadership potential within the team.
- **Performance Metrics**: Implement systems to track and evaluate productivity.

3. Expand Horizons

- **Market Research**: Identify opportunities in international markets.

- **Strategic Alliances**: Form partnerships with global entities.
- **Cultural Competence Training**: Prepare teams for international engagement.

4. Embrace Counsel and Legacy Planning

- **Open Dialogue**: Foster an environment where feedback is encouraged and valued.
- **Succession Planning**: Develop clear plans for leadership transitions.
- **Preserve Core Values**: Ensure that organizational values are maintained over time.

5. Maintain Ethical Standards

- **Code of Ethics**: Develop and enforce a comprehensive code of conduct.
- **Ethics Training**: Provide regular training on ethical issues relevant to the industry.
- **Transparency**: Be open with stakeholders about practices and policies.

Conclusion

King Solomon's reign offers a wealth of insights into effective leadership, strategic planning, and the complexities of wealth accumulation. By prioritizing wisdom, establishing efficient administrative structures, engaging in international trade, and heeding wise counsel, modern businesses can emulate the aspects of Solomon's model that led to prosperity and renown. However, his later failures also serve as cautionary tales about the dangers of complacency and ethical lapses. By learning from both his successes and mistakes, we can strive to build businesses that are not only successful but also grounded in wisdom and integrity.

Reflection Questions

1. **Wisdom in Leadership**: How are you prioritizing wisdom and understanding in your leadership approach?
2. **Organizational Efficiency**: What steps can you take to improve delegation and resource management in your business?
3. **Global Opportunities**: Are there international markets or partnerships that could enhance your business? How can you pursue them?
4. **Heeding Advice**: Do you actively seek and value counsel from experienced advisors? How can you improve in this area?
5. **Ethical Vigilance**: What measures are in place to ensure that your business maintains high ethical standards?

Key Scriptures for Further Reflection

- **1 Kings 3:9**: Solomon's request for wisdom.
- **1 Kings 4:7**: Solomon's administrative organization.
- **1 Kings 10:1-13**: The Queen of Sheba's visit and Solomon's wealth.
- **2 Chronicles 10:8**: Rehoboam's rejection of wise counsel.
- **Proverbs 4:7**: The importance of wisdom.
- **Proverbs 11:14**: The value of multiple counselors.
- **Ecclesiastes 11:2**: Diversification.
- **Mark 8:36**: The profit of gaining the world but losing one's soul.

End of Chapter 4

CHAPTER 5: THE MODEL OF SERVANT LEADERSHIP

"For even the Son of Man did not come to be served, but to serve."
— *Mark 10:45*

Introduction

Traditional leadership models often emphasize authority, control, and a top-down hierarchy. However, the concept of servant leadership, rooted in biblical principles, offers a transformative approach that prioritizes serving others over exerting power. This model turns conventional leadership on its head by suggesting that leaders achieve the greatest influence not by demanding service, but by serving others themselves. This chapter explores the principles of servant leadership, its benefits to organizational culture, and practical ways to implement it within modern businesses.

Principles of Servant Leadership

Definition Of Servant Leadership

Servant leadership is a philosophy where the main goal of the leader is to serve. This is different from traditional leadership, where the leader's focus is the thriving of their company or organization. Servant leaders prioritize the needs of their team members and organization before their own.

Biblical Foundation

Jesus Christ exemplifies servant leadership throughout the New Testament. In *Mark 10:45*, He states:

"For even the Son of Man did not come to be served, but to serve."

Core Principles

1. **Empathy**

    - **Understanding Others**: Servant leaders strive to understand and empathize with others' feelings and perspectives.
    - **Active Listening**: They pay attention to the needs and concerns of their team members.

2. **Humility**

    - **Selflessness**: Putting the needs of others before one's own ego or ambitions.
    - **Acknowledging Limitations**: Recognizing personal

weaknesses and being open to input from others.

3. **Stewardship**

   - **Responsible Management**: Caring for the organization's resources and people as a steward rather than an owner.
   - **Accountability**: Taking responsibility for the team's successes and failures.

4. **Empowerment**

   - **Facilitating Growth**: Encouraging personal and professional development among team members.
   - **Delegation**: Trusting others with responsibilities and authority.

5. **Vision**

   - **Forward-Thinking**: Having a clear direction and purpose that aligns with the organization's values.
   - **Inspiration**: Motivating others by sharing a compelling vision.

Biblical Insight

- **Jesus Washing the Disciples' Feet**

   In *John 13:14-15*, Jesus washes His disciples' feet, an act of humility and service.

   "If I then, your Lord and Teacher, have washed your feet, you also ought to wash one another's feet."

Benefits to Organizational Culture

Enhanced Employee Engagement

- **Increased Morale**: Employees feel valued and respected, leading to higher job satisfaction.
- **Loyalty**: A supportive environment fosters loyalty and reduces turnover rates.

Improved Collaboration

- **Team Cohesion**: Servant leadership promotes a culture of trust and openness.
- **Effective Communication**: Encourages honest dialogue and feedback.

Greater Innovation

- **Empowered Employees**: Team members are more likely to contribute ideas when they feel their input is valued.
- **Risk-Taking**: A supportive environment encourages calculated risks, leading to innovation.

Customer Satisfaction

- **Customer-Centric Focus**: Servant leaders often extend

their service mindset to customers, enhancing customer relationships.
- **Quality Improvement**: A committed team is more attentive to delivering high-quality products or services.

Ethical Workplace

- **Integrity**: Servant leaders model ethical behavior, setting a standard for the organization.
- **Accountability**: Promotes a culture where ethical breaches are less likely to occur.

Biblical Insight

- **"Do nothing out of selfish ambition or vain conceit. Rather, in humility value others above yourselves."** — *Philippians 2:3*

mplementing Servant Leadership Practices

1. Develop a Servant Leadership Mindset

  - **Self-Reflection**
  - Assess personal leadership style and openness to change.
  - Identify areas where serving others can be prioritized.

Commitment To Personal Growth

- Engage in continuous learning about servant leadership principles.
  - Seek mentorship or coaching if necessary.

2. Prioritize the Needs of Employees

- **Active Listening**

  - Hold regular one-on-one meetings to understand team members' needs and concerns.
  - Encourage open communication without fear of retribution.

- **Provide Support**

  - Offer resources and assistance to help employees succeed.
  - Recognize and address personal or professional challenges they may face.

3. Empower and Develop Others

- **Delegation with Trust**

  - Assign tasks that challenge employees and help them grow.
  - Trust them to make decisions and provide autonomy.

- **Professional Development**

  - Invest in training and educational opportunities.
  - Create clear pathways for career advancement.

4. Model Ethical and Caring Behavior

- **Lead by Example**

  - Demonstrate integrity in all actions.
  - Show respect and kindness in interactions.

- **Accountability**

  - Admit mistakes openly and take responsibility.
  - Encourage a culture where mistakes are viewed as learning opportunities.

5. Foster a Collaborative Environment

- **Team Building**

  - Organize activities that strengthen team relationships.
  - Encourage collaboration over competition.

- **Inclusive Decision-Making**

  - Involve team members in decisions that affect them.
  - Value diverse perspectives and ideas.

6. Communicate a Clear Vision

- **Share the Mission**

  - Ensure everyone understands the organization's purpose and goals.
  - Connect individual roles to the larger mission.

- **Inspire And Motivate**

- Use storytelling and real-life examples to illustrate the vision.
- Recognize and celebrate achievements towards the vision.

Biblical Insight

- **"Each of you should use whatever gift you have received to serve others."** — *1 Peter 4:10*

Case Studies of Servant Leadership in Business

Case Study 1: Southwest Airlines

- **Employee Focus**

  - Puts employees first, believing that satisfied employees will lead to satisfied customers.
  - Encourages a fun and supportive work environment.

- **Results**

  - High employee retention rates.
  - Strong customer loyalty and consistent profitability.

Case Study 2: Starbucks

- **Inclusive Culture**

  - Provides comprehensive benefits and education opportunities to employees ("partners").
  - Emphasizes respect and dignity in the workplace.

- **Results**

- Enhanced brand reputation.
- Engaged workforce contributing to innovation and customer satisfaction.

Case Study 3: The Container Store

- **Communication and Transparency**

  - Practices open-book management, sharing financial information with employees.
  - Invests heavily in employee training and development.

- **Results**

  - Recognized as one of the best companies to work for.
  - Strong financial performance and customer service excellence.

Challenges and Solutions in Adopting Servant Leadership

Challenge 1: Resistance To Change

- **Solution**

  - Start small by introducing servant leadership principles gradually.
  - Highlight the benefits through pilot programs or departments.

Challenge 2: Balancing Service And Authority

- **Solution**

  - Understand that serving others does not mean relinquishing authority.
  - Maintain clear boundaries and expectations while supporting the team.

Challenge 3: Short-Term Pressure

- **Solution**

  - Communicate the long-term benefits of servant leadership to stakeholders.
  - Align servant leadership practices with strategic objectives.

Practical Steps for Leaders

Self-Assessment

- **Identify Strengths and Weaknesses**

  - Use tools like 360-degree feedback to gain insight.
  - Reflect on how current practices align with servant leadership.

Set Clear Goals

- **Develop an Action Plan**

  - Outline specific steps to incorporate servant leadership.
  - Set measurable objectives and timelines.

Seek Feedback and Adjust

- **Continuous Improvement**

  - Regularly solicit feedback from team members.
  - Be willing to adjust strategies based on input.

Mentorship and Training

- **Lead by Example**

  - Mentor emerging leaders in servant leadership principles.
  - Provide training opportunities for the entire team.

Conclusion

Adopting the model of servant leadership can transform an organization's culture, driving engagement, innovation, and ethical behavior. By prioritizing the needs of employees and customers, leaders create an environment where individuals feel valued and motivated to contribute their best efforts. This approach aligns with the biblical example set by Jesus, emphasizing humility, service, and love for others. Implementing servant leadership is not without challenges, but the long-term benefits to organizational health and performance make it a worthwhile endeavor.

Reflection Questions

1. **Personal Leadership Style**: In what ways does your current leadership style reflect servant leadership principles? Where can you improve?
2. **Employee Engagement**: How can you better serve your team to enhance their engagement and productivity?
3. **Organizational Culture**: What steps can you take to foster a culture of service within your organization?

Key Scriptures for Further Reflection

- **Mark 10:45**: Jesus came to serve, not to be served.
- **John 13:14-15**: Jesus washes the disciples' feet.
- **Philippians 2:3-4**: Valuing others above oneself.
- **1 Peter 4:10**: Using gifts to serve others.
- **Matthew 20:26-28**: The greatest must be a servant.

End of Chapter 5

CHAPTER 6: WEALTH, MONEY, AND ETHICAL PROFIT

"For the love of money is a root of all kinds of evil." — *1 Timothy 6:10*

Introduction

Money plays an indispensable role in the functioning of any business. It serves as a medium of exchange, a unit of account, and a store of value. However, the Bible cautions against allowing money to become an idol or the primary focus of one's life. In *1 Timothy 6:10*, we are warned that the love of money can lead to various evils. This chapter explores how businesses can pursue profit ethically, use wealth as a tool for good, and avoid the pitfalls of greed. By aligning financial goals with ethical standards, businesses can achieve success that is both profitable and principled.

Ethical Considerations in Profit-Making

Understanding The Role Of Money

Money itself is neutral—a tool that can be used for good or ill. The issue arises when the pursuit of money becomes an end rather than a means.

Biblical Insight

 - **"No one can serve two masters... You cannot serve God and mammon."** — *Matthew 6:24*

This verse emphasizes that an obsession with wealth can distract from higher moral and spiritual obligations.

Principles for Ethical Profit-Making

1. **Integrity in Transactions**

   - **Honest Practices**: Conduct business dealings transparently without deception or fraud.

   - **"A false balance is an abomination to the LORD, but a just weight is his delight."** — *Proverbs 11:1*

   - **Fair Pricing**: Set prices that are fair to both the company and the customer, avoiding exploitation.

2. **Quality of Products and Services**

   - **Excellence**: Deliver products or services that meet or exceed expectations.

- **Safety and Compliance**: Adhere to regulations and standards to ensure the well-being of consumers.

3. **Respect for Stakeholders**

   - **Employees**: Provide fair wages, safe working conditions, and opportunities for growth.

   - **"Do not withhold good from those to whom it is due, when it is in your power to act."** — *Proverbs 3:27*

   - **Suppliers and Partners**: Engage in fair contracts and honor commitments.

4. **Social Responsibility**

   - **Environmental Stewardship**: Implement sustainable practices to protect the environment.

   - **Community Engagement**: Contribute positively to the communities in which the business operates.

5. **Transparency and Accountability**

   - **Open Communication**: Be honest with stakeholders about business practices and financials.

   - **Ethical Governance**: Establish policies that promote ethical behavior at all levels.

Benefits Of Ethical Profit-Making

- **Reputation Management**: Builds trust with customers,

investors, and the public.

- **Employee Morale**: Enhances job satisfaction and loyalty among employees.

- **Long-Term Success**: Ethical businesses are more likely to sustain profitability over time.

Philanthropy and Giving Back

Biblical Foundation for Generosity

Generosity is a recurring theme in the Bible, encouraging believers to use their resources to help others.

- **"Command them to do good, to be rich in good deeds, and to be generous and willing to share."** — *1 Timothy 6:18*

Ways Businesses Can Give Back

1. **Financial Donations**

   - **Charitable Contributions**: Allocate a portion of profits to support non-profit organizations and causes.

   - **Matching Programs**: Match employees' charitable donations to amplify impact.

2. **Community Investment**

- **Local Development**: Invest in projects that improve community infrastructure and services.

   - **Education and Training**: Support schools, scholarships, and vocational training programs.

3. **Employee Volunteerism**

   - **Volunteer Programs**: Encourage and facilitate employee participation in community service.

   - **Paid Volunteer Days**: Offer paid time off for employees to volunteer.

4. **Pro Bono Services**

   - **Professional Expertise**: Provide services free of charge to non-profits or underserved populations.

5. **Sustainable Practices**

   - **Environmental Initiatives**: Implement practices that reduce environmental impact, benefiting society as a whole.

Impact Of Philanthropy

- **Social Good**: Addresses societal needs and contributes to the well-being of communities.

- **Enhanced Brand Image**: Positively influences public perception and customer loyalty.

- **Employee Engagement**: Increases job satisfaction and

retention by fostering a sense of purpose.

Biblical Insight

- *"Whoever is generous to the poor lends to the LORD, and he will repay him for his deed."* — *Proverbs 19:17*

Avoiding the Pitfalls of Greed

Understanding Greed

Greed is an excessive desire for more than is needed or deserved, especially regarding wealth.

- **Biblical Warning**

  - *"Then he said to them, 'Watch out! Be on your guard against all kinds of greed; life does not consist in an abundance of possessions.'"* — *Luke 12:15*

Consequences Of Greed In Business

1. **Ethical Compromise**

   - **Cutting Corners**: Sacrificing quality or safety to reduce costs.

- **Dishonest Practices**: Engaging in fraud, corruption, or exploitation.

2. **Damaged Relationships**

   - **Customer Distrust**: Losing customers due to unethical behavior.

   - **Employee Dissatisfaction**: High turnover rates when employees feel undervalued or exploited.

3. **Legal Repercussions**

   - **Fines and Penalties**: Facing legal action for violating laws and regulations.

   - **Loss of Licenses**: Potentially losing the right to operate.

4. **Reputation Damage**

   - **Public Backlash**: Negative publicity can lead to long-term brand damage.

   - **Investor Withdrawal**: Loss of investor confidence can impact capital and growth.

Strategies To Avoid Greed

1. **Set Ethical Standards**

   - **Code of Conduct**: Establish clear guidelines for ethical behavior.

   - **Leadership Example**: Leaders should model integrity and selflessness.

2. **Define Success Holistically**

   - **Beyond Profit**: Incorporate social and environmental goals into the definition of success.

   - **Balanced Scorecard**: Use metrics that measure financial, customer, internal process, and learning and growth perspectives.

3. **Accountability Mechanisms**

   - **Audits and Oversight**: Regularly review practices to ensure compliance with ethical standards.

   - **Whistleblower Policies**: Encourage reporting of unethical behavior without fear of retaliation.

4. **Foster a Culture of Contentment**

   - **Gratitude Practices**: Encourage reflection on achievements and appreciation for current resources.

   - **Employee Well-being**: Prioritize work-life balance and mental health.

Biblical Insight

- **"Keep your lives free from the love of money and be content with what you have."** — *Hebrews 13:5*

Case Studies of Ethical

Case Study 1: Patagonia

- **Environmental Commitment**

  - **1% for the Planet**: Donates 1% of sales to environmental causes.

  - **Sustainable Products**: Focuses on creating durable, eco-friendly products.

- **Impact**

  - **Customer Loyalty**: Attracts customers who value sustainability.

  - **Industry Influence**: Sets standards for environmental responsibility in retail.

Case Study 2: Ben & Jerry's

- **Social Mission**

  - **Fair Trade Ingredients**: Sources ingredients that support fair wages and sustainable farming.

  - **Advocacy**: Actively engages in social justice campaigns.

- **Impact**

- **Brand Differentiation**: Stands out in the market due to strong ethical stance.

   - **Employee Engagement**: High levels of employee satisfaction and retention.

Case Study 3: The Body Shop

- **Ethical Practices**

   - **Against Animal Testing**: Pioneered cruelty-free beauty products.

   - **Community Trade**: Sources ingredients from marginalized communities to promote fair trade.

- **Impact**

   - **Global Recognition**: Known worldwide for ethical standards.

   - **Sustainable Growth**: Achieved financial success while maintaining ethical commitments.

Balancing Profit and Purpose

Integrating Ethics Into Business Models

- **Social Enterprises**

  - **Dual Objectives**: Combine profit-making with social impact.

  - **Examples**: Companies that reinvest profits into community development.

- **Triple Bottom Line**

  - **People, Planet, Profit**: Measures success based on social, environmental, and financial performance.

Steps To Achieve Balance

1. **Mission Alignment**

   - **Define Core Values**: Articulate the ethical principles that guide the business.

   - **Align Strategies**: Ensure that business strategies reflect these values.

2. **Stakeholder Engagement**

   - **Inclusive Decision-Making**: Consider the impact on all stakeholders, including employees, customers, suppliers, and the community.

 - **Feedback Mechanisms**: Create channels for stakeholder input and concerns.

3. **Transparent Reporting**

 - **Sustainability Reports**: Publish reports on social and environmental performance.

 - **Financial Transparency**: Provide clear and honest financial disclosures.

Biblical Insight

- **"But seek first the kingdom of God and His righteousness, and all these things shall be added to you."** — *Matthew 6:33*

Practical Steps for Ethical Wealth Management

1. Establish Ethical Guidelines

- **Develop a Code of Ethics**

 - Outline expectations for behavior and decision-making.

- **Train Employees**

 - Provide regular training on ethical standards and practices.

2. Implement Ethical Business Practices

- **Fair Trade Policies**

   - Engage in fair pricing and labor practices throughout the supply chain.

- **Quality Assurance**

   - Commit to high standards for products and services.

3. Foster a Generous Corporate Culture

- **Encourage Philanthropy**

   - Set up programs for charitable giving and volunteerism.

- **Reward Ethical Behavior**

   - Recognize and reward employees who exemplify ethical standards.

4. Monitor and Evaluate

- **Regular Audits**

   - Conduct internal and external audits to ensure compliance.

- **Performance Metrics**

   - Use key performance indicators (KPIs) that include ethical and social considerations.

5. Engage in Continuous Improvement

- **Stay Informed**

- Keep abreast of best practices in ethical business conduct.

- **Adapt and Innovate**

- Be willing to change policies and practices in response to new information or societal shifts.

Conclusion

Wealth and profit are not inherently negative; they become problematic when pursued without regard for ethical standards and the well-being of others. By viewing money as a tool rather than an idol, businesses can achieve financial success while contributing positively to society. Ethical profit-making involves integrity, generosity, and a conscious effort to avoid the trappings of greed. Aligning business practices with biblical principles ensures that wealth serves a greater purpose, benefiting not only the organization but also its stakeholders and the broader community.

Reflection Questions

1. **Ethical Alignment**: How does your organization's pursuit of profit align with its ethical standards and core values?

2. **Philanthropic Efforts**: In what ways can your business give back to the community or support social causes?

3. **Preventing Greed**: What measures can you implement to avoid the pitfalls of greed within your organization?

*Key Scriptures for
Further Reflection*

- **1 Timothy 6:10**: The love of money as a root of all kinds of evil.
- **Matthew 6:24**: Serving God versus serving money.
- **Hebrews 13:5**: Contentment and freedom from the love of money.
- **Proverbs 11:1**: Honest scales and delighting the Lord.
- **Luke 12:15**: Warning against greed.
- **Matthew 6:33**: Seeking first the kingdom of God.

End of Chapter 6

CHAPTER 7: JUSTICE AND FAIRNESS IN THE MARKETPLACE

"He has shown you, O man, what is good; and what does the LORD require of you but to do justly..." — *Micah 6:8*

Introduction

Justice and fairness are foundational principles that underpin a healthy and prosperous society. In the realm of business, these values are essential for fostering trust, loyalty, and long-term success. The Bible emphasizes the importance of acting justly in all dealings, reminding us that ethical conduct is not optional but a divine requirement. This chapter explores how businesses can implement fair policies in their interactions with employees, customers, and competitors, and how they can contribute to a just economy through advocacy and responsible practices.

Fair Labor Practices

Biblical Foundation

- **"Do not exploit a hired worker who is poor and needy, whether one of your fellow Israelites or a foreigner residing in your towns."** — *Deuteronomy 24:14*
- **"The laborer deserves his wages."** — *Luke 10:7*

Principles Of Fair Labor

1. **Fair Compensation**

   - **Living Wages**: Ensure that employees receive wages sufficient to meet basic living standards.
   - **Equal Pay for Equal Work**: Eliminate wage disparities based on gender, race, or other discriminatory factors.

2. **Safe Working Conditions**

   - **Health and Safety Standards**: Comply with or exceed industry regulations to protect employees from harm.
   - **Workplace Environment**: Promote a culture of respect, free from harassment and discrimination.

3. **Respect for Workers' Rights**

   - **Freedom of Association**: Allow employees to form or join unions without fear of retaliation.
   - **Reasonable Working Hours**: Avoid excessive overtime and provide adequate rest periods.

4. **Opportunities for Growth**

- **Training and Development**: Invest in employee skills and career advancement.
  - **Recognition and Reward**: Acknowledge contributions and offer incentives for high performance.

Application In Business

- **Policy Implementation**: Develop comprehensive labor policies that reflect fair practices and adhere to legal standards.
- **Auditing and Compliance**: Regularly review labor practices to ensure ongoing compliance and address any issues promptly.
- **Employee Engagement**: Create channels for open communication, allowing employees to voice concerns and suggestions.

Benefits Of Fair Labor Practices

- **Increased Productivity**: Satisfied employees are more motivated and productive.
- **Employee Retention**: Fair treatment reduces turnover, saving costs on recruitment and training.
- **Positive Reputation**: Attracts talent and builds trust with customers and the community.

Biblical Insight

- ***"Masters, treat your bondservants justly and fairly, knowing that you also have a Master in heaven."*** — *Colossians 4:1*

Equitable Treatment of Customers

Biblical Foundation

- **"So in everything, do to others what you would have them do to you."** — *Matthew 7:12*
- **"A just balance and scales are the Lord's; all the weights in the bag are his work."** — *Proverbs 16:11*

Principles Of Fair Customer Relations

1. **Honest Communication**

   - **Transparent Pricing**: Clearly disclose all costs and fees associated with products or services.
   - **Truthful Marketing**: Avoid deceptive advertising and ensure that all claims are accurate.

2. **Quality Assurance**

   - **Product Integrity**: Deliver products and services that meet or exceed quality standards.
   - **After-Sales Support**: Provide warranties, returns, and customer service that address customer needs.

3. **Non-Discrimination**

   - **Equal Access**: Serve all customers regardless of race, gender, religion, or other characteristics.

- **Accessibility**: Make accommodations for customers with disabilities.

4. **Data Privacy**

   - **Protecting Personal Information**: Safeguard customer data and use it responsibly.
   - **Consent and Transparency**: Be clear about data collection practices and obtain necessary permissions.

Application In Business

- **Customer Service Training**: Equip staff with the skills to handle customer interactions professionally.
- **Feedback Mechanisms**: Encourage and facilitate customer feedback to improve services.
- **Fair Policies**: Establish policies that are customer-centric and fair, such as return and refund policies.

Benefits Of Equitable Treatment

- **Customer Loyalty**: Fair and respectful treatment fosters repeat business.
- **Brand Reputation**: Builds trust and a positive image in the marketplace.
- **Competitive Advantage**: Differentiates the business through exceptional customer care.

Biblical Insight

- **"Better is a little with righteousness than great revenues with injustice."** — *Proverbs 16:8*

Advocacy for Justice in Industry Regulations

Biblical Foundation

- **"Speak up for those who cannot speak for themselves, for the rights of all who are destitute."** — *Proverbs 31:8*

Principles of Advocacy

1. **Ethical Leadership**

    - **Role Modeling**: Demonstrate commitment to justice through business practices.
    - **Influencing Industry Standards**: Advocate for ethical norms within the industry.

2. **Policy Engagement**

    - **Regulatory Participation**: Engage with policymakers to shape fair regulations.
    - **Compliance and Beyond**: Not only meet but exceed legal requirements for ethical conduct.

3. **Collaboration**

   - **Industry Coalitions**: Join forces with other businesses to promote justice.
   - **Community Partnerships**: Work with NGOs and community groups to address social issues.

4. **Transparency**

   - **Public Reporting**: Share information about business practices and impact openly.
   - **Accountability Mechanisms**: Implement systems to hold the company accountable for its actions.

Application in Business

- **Corporate Social Responsibility (CSR)**: Integrate social and environmental concerns into business operations.
- **Advocacy Programs**: Support initiatives that promote justice and fairness in the industry.
- **Ethics Committees**: Establish internal bodies to oversee ethical practices and policies.

Benefits of Advocacy

- **Social Impact**: Contribute to positive change in society and the economy.
- **Reputation Enhancement**: Gain recognition as a leader in ethical business practices.
- **Risk Mitigation**: Proactively addressing issues can prevent future legal or reputational problems.

Biblical Insight

- **"Learn to do right; seek justice. Defend the oppressed."** — *Isaiah 1:17*

Practical Steps to Promote Justice and Fairness

1. Conduct Ethical Audits

  - **Assess Current Practices**: Identify areas where the business may fall short in justice and fairness.
  - **Set Improvement Goals**: Develop action plans to address deficiencies.

2. Develop and Implement Fair Policies

  - **Employee Policies**: Ensure all HR policies promote fairness and equal opportunity.
  - **Customer Policies**: Review terms and conditions to eliminate any unfair provisions.

3. Foster an Inclusive Culture

  - **Diversity Initiatives**: Promote diversity in hiring and leadership.
  - **Training Programs**: Educate employees on unconscious bias and inclusive practices.

4. Engage in Ethical Supply Chain Management

  - **Supplier Standards**: Require fair labor practices from suppliers and contractors.
  - **Supply Chain Transparency**: Trace and disclose the origins of products and materials.

5. Participate in Community Development

   - **Local Hiring**: Create job opportunities in the communities where the business operates.
   - **Support Education and Training**: Invest in programs that enhance skills and employability.

6. Advocate for Fair Regulations

   - **Policy Advocacy**: Support laws and regulations that promote justice and fairness.
   - **Public Awareness**: Use the company's platform to raise awareness about social justice issues.

Case Studies of Justice and Fairness in Business

Case Study 1: Toms Shoes

  -**One for One Model**

  - **Social Impact**: For every pair of shoes sold, TOMS donates a pair to a child in need.
     - **Fair Practices**: Ensures ethical labor practices in manufacturing.

  - **Impact**
  - **Global Reach**: Has donated millions of shoes worldwide.
     - **Customer Engagement**: Attracts customers who value social responsibility.

Case Study 2: Microsoft

  - **Diversity and Inclusion**
  - **Equal Opportunity**: Implements programs to increase diversity at all levels.
  - **Pay Equity**: Actively works to eliminate wage gaps.
  - **Impact**

    - **Innovative Culture**: Diverse teams contribute to innovation.
    - **Industry Leadership**: Sets a standard for other tech companies.

Case Study 3: Ben & Jerry's

- **Advocacy for Social Justice**

  - **Public Stance**: Actively campaigns for social issues like climate justice and LGBTQ+ rights.
  - **Fair Trade Ingredients**: Sources ingredients ethically to support fair labor practices.

- **Impact**

  - **Brand Loyalty**: Builds a strong connection with customers who share similar values.
  - **Positive Change**: Contributes to societal conversations and policy changes.

Conclusion

Justice and fairness are essential components of ethical business practices. By upholding fair labor practices, treating customers equitably, and advocating for just regulations, businesses not only comply with moral and legal standards but also build a foundation for sustainable success. These principles foster trust, loyalty, and a positive reputation, which are invaluable assets in today's competitive marketplace. Aligning business operations with the biblical mandate to "do justly" ensures that companies contribute positively to society and reflect the values that promote the common good.

Reflection Questions

1. **Assessing Fairness**: In what areas can your business improve its commitment to justice and fairness?
2. **Employee Engagement**: How can you better support fair labor practices within your organization?
3. **Community Involvement**: What role can your business play in advocating for justice in your industry or community?

Key Scriptures for Further Reflection

- **Micah 6:8**: Acting justly as a divine requirement.
- **Proverbs 16:11**: God's delight in honest scales and fairness.
- **Isaiah 1:17**: The call to defend the oppressed and seek justice.
- **James 5:4**: Warning against exploiting workers.

- **Matthew 7:12**: The Golden Rule in treating others.

End of Chapter 7

CHAPTER 8: THE IMPORTANCE OF VISION AND PLANNING

"Where there is no vision, the people perish." — *Proverbs 29:18*

Introduction

A clear and compelling vision is the cornerstone of any successful enterprise. It serves as a guiding light, directing the organization's path and inspiring stakeholders to work towards common goals. In the Bible, the significance of vision is emphasized in *Proverbs 29:18*, highlighting that without it, people lose direction and purpose. This chapter delves into the critical role of vision and strategic planning in business, exploring how crafting a mission statement, balancing long-term and short-term planning, and aligning company goals with ethical values can lead to sustained success and fulfillment.

Crafting a Mission Statement

Defining The Mission Statement

A mission statement is a concise declaration of an organization's core purpose and focus. It communicates what the company does, whom it serves, and how it serves them. A well-crafted mission statement encapsulates the organization's identity and sets the tone for its culture and operations.

Biblical Foundation

  - **Clarity of Purpose**
  - **"Write the vision and make it plain on tablets, that he may run who reads it."** — *Habakkuk 2:2*

This verse underscores the importance of articulating the vision clearly so that those who read it can act upon it effectively.

Elements Of An Effective Mission Statement

1. **Purpose**

   - **What We Do**: Clearly state the primary products or services offered.
   - **Why We Do It**: Explain the underlying reasons or motivations.

2. **Values**

   - **Core Principles**: Reflect the ethical standards and beliefs that guide the organization's actions.

3. **Audience**

   - **Whom We Serve**: Identify the primary stakeholders, such as customers, employees, and the community.

4. **Commitment**

   - **Dedication to Excellence**: Express a commitment to quality and continuous improvement.

Steps to Craft a Mission Statement

1. **Reflect on Core Values**

   - **Identify Beliefs**: Determine the ethical principles that are non-negotiable.
   - **Biblical Alignment**: Ensure values are consistent with biblical teachings.

2. **Engage Stakeholders**

   - **Inclusive Process**: Involve employees, leadership, and even customers in the development process.
   - **Diverse Perspectives**: Incorporate insights from various levels of the organization.

3. **Keep it Concise**

   - **Simplicity**: Aim for clarity and brevity to make the mission statement memorable.
   - **Avoid Jargon**: Use language that is accessible to all stakeholders.

4. **Review and Revise**

- **Feedback Loop**: Seek input and be willing to make adjustments.
   - **Periodic Updates**: Revisit the mission statement as the organization evolves.

Application In Business

- **Guiding Decisions**

  - **Strategic Alignment**: Use the mission statement to evaluate new opportunities and initiatives.
  - **Resource Allocation**: Prioritize projects that support the core mission.

- **Motivating Employees**

  - **Sense of Purpose**: Help employees understand how their roles contribute to the larger vision.
  - **Cultural Cohesion**: Foster a shared identity and collective commitment.

Biblical Insight

- *"For I know the plans I have for you, declares the LORD, plans to prosper you and not to harm you, plans to give you hope and a future."* — *Jeremiah 29:11*

Just as God has a plan for His people, organizations should have a clear plan that offers hope and direction.

Long-Term versus Short-Term Planning

The Balance Between Now And The Future

Effective planning requires balancing immediate needs with future goals. While short-term planning addresses current challenges and opportunities, long-term planning focuses on sustainable growth and adaptation.

Biblical Foundation

- **Forethought and Preparation**

  - *"Suppose one of you wants to build a tower. Won't you first sit down and estimate the cost to see if you have enough money to complete it?"* — *Luke 14:28*

  This passage highlights the importance of considering the full scope of a project before embarking on it.

Short-Term Planning

- **Characteristics**

- **Time Frame**: Typically covers a period of up to one year.
  - **Objectives**: Focuses on immediate operational goals and problem-solving.

- **Importance**

  - **Agility**: Allows the organization to respond quickly to market changes.
  - **Resource Management**: Addresses current financial and human resource needs.

Long-Term Planning

- **Characteristics**

  - **Time Frame**: Encompasses several years into the future.
  - **Objectives**: Centers on strategic goals, growth, and sustainability.

- **Importance**

  - **Vision Realization**: Aligns with the mission statement to achieve overarching goals.
  - **Risk Management**: Anticipates future challenges and prepares accordingly.

Integrating Both Planning Horizons

1. **Set Clear Goals**

   - **SMART Objectives**: Ensure goals are Specific, Measurable,

Achievable, Relevant, and Time-bound.
   - **Alignment**: Short-term goals should be stepping stones toward long-term objectives.

2. **Flexible Strategies**

   - **Adaptability**: Be prepared to adjust plans in response to new information or circumstances.
   - **Continuous Monitoring**: Regularly review progress and make necessary adjustments.

3. **Resource Allocation**

   - **Balanced Investment**: Allocate resources in a way that supports both immediate operations and future growth.

Application In Business

- **Strategic Roadmaps**

   - **Milestones**: Define key milestones that connect short-term actions to long-term goals.
   - **Performance Indicators**: Use metrics to track progress and inform decision-making.

- **Stakeholder Communication**

   - **Transparency**: Share plans with stakeholders to build trust and secure support.
   - **Engagement**: Involve stakeholders in planning processes to gain valuable insights.

Biblical Insight

- **"The plans of the diligent lead surely to abundance, but everyone who is hasty comes only to poverty."** — *Proverbs 21:5*

Diligent planning contributes to success, while rash actions can lead to failure.

Aligning Company Goals with Ethical Values

The Role Of Ethics In Business Planning

Aligning company goals with ethical values ensures that the organization's actions are consistent with its core principles. This alignment fosters integrity, builds reputation, and contributes to long-term success.

Biblical Foundation

- **Integrity and Righteousness**

  - **"Better is a little with righteousness than great revenues with injustice."** — *Proverbs 16:8*

This verse emphasizes that ethical conduct is more valuable than wealth gained through unethical means.

Strategies For Alignment

1. **Define Ethical Standards**

    - **Core Values Statement**: Articulate the ethical principles that guide the organization.
    - **Code of Conduct**: Establish policies that reflect these values in day-to-day operations.

2. **Incorporate Ethics into Goals**

    - **Goal Setting**: Ensure that strategic objectives do not compromise ethical standards.
    - **Decision-Making Framework**: Use ethical considerations as a criterion for evaluating options.

3. **Leadership Commitment**

    - **Modeling Behavior**: Leaders should exemplify ethical conduct in all actions.
    - **Accountability**: Establish mechanisms to hold everyone in the organization accountable.

4. **Stakeholder Consideration**

    - **Impact Assessment**: Evaluate how goals affect employees, customers, community, and environment.
    - **Engagement**: Seek input from stakeholders to understand their values and expectations.

Application In Business

- **Ethical Business Practices**

    - **Fair Trade**: Engage in practices that promote fairness in the supply chain.
    - **Corporate Social Responsibility (CSR)**: Implement initiatives that benefit society and the environment.

- **Risk Management**

    - **Reputation Protection**: Ethical alignment reduces the risk of scandals and legal issues.
    - **Sustainable Growth**: Builds a loyal customer base and attracts quality employees.

Biblical Insight

- **"Whoever walks in integrity walks securely, but he who makes his ways crooked will be found out."** — *Proverbs 10:9*

   Acting with integrity provides security, while unethical behavior leads to exposure and consequences.

Practical Steps for Implementing Vision and Planning

1. Engage in Strategic Planning Sessions

   - **Collaborative Approach**: Involve key team members in developing plans.
   - **SWOT Analysis**: Assess Strengths, Weaknesses, Opportunities, and Threats.

2. Communicate the Vision

   - **Internal Communication**: Ensure all employees understand and embrace the vision.
   - **External Communication**: Share the vision with customers and partners to build alignment.

3. Monitor and Evaluate Progress

   - **Regular Reviews**: Schedule periodic assessments of progress toward goals.
   - **Adjustments**: Be willing to refine plans in response to changing circumstances.

4. Foster a Culture of Vision

   - **Training and Development**: Provide resources to help employees align with the vision.
   - **Recognition and Rewards**: Acknowledge contributions that advance the organization's goals.

Case Studies of Vision and Planning

Case Study 1: Apple Inc.

- **Visionary Leadership**

  - **Steve Jobs' Vision**: Focused on innovation and creating user-friendly technology.
  - **Mission Statement**: Emphasized empowering individuals through technology.

- **Strategic Planning**

  - **Long-Term Innovation**: Invested in research and development for future products.
  - **Brand Alignment**: Ensured that all products and marketing efforts reflected core values.

Impact

- **Market Leadership**: Became a leading company in consumer electronics.
- **Customer Loyalty**: Built a strong, devoted customer base.

Case Study 2: Patagonia

- **Mission Statement**

  - **"We're in business to save our home planet."**

  - **Ethical Alignment**
  - **Environmental Stewardship**: Incorporated sustainability into all aspects of the business.
  - **Corporate Activism**: Advocated for environmental policies and donated to related causes.

Impact

- **Brand Reputation**: Recognized as a leader in ethical business practices.
- **Financial Success**: Achieved profitability while adhering to ethical principles.

Conclusion

Vision and planning are not merely administrative tasks; they are fundamental to an organization's identity and success. A clear vision provides direction and purpose, while strategic planning bridges the gap between where the organization is and where it aims to be. By crafting a mission statement, balancing short-term and long-term planning, and aligning goals with ethical values, businesses can navigate the complexities of the marketplace with confidence and integrity. Rooted in biblical wisdom, these principles guide organizations toward sustainable success that benefits all stakeholders.

Reflection Questions

1. **Mission Clarity**: Does your organization have a clear and compelling mission statement? How well does it reflect your core values?

2. **Planning Balance**: How effectively are you balancing short-term needs with long-term goals in your planning processes?

3. **Ethical Alignment**: In what ways are your company's goals aligned with ethical principles? Where can improvements be made?

Key Scriptures for Further Reflection

- **Proverbs 29:18**: The necessity of vision.
- **Habakkuk 2:2**: Writing and communicating the vision clearly.
- **Luke 14:28**: The importance of planning and counting the cost.
- **Proverbs 21:5**: The benefits of diligent planning.
- **Proverbs 16:8**: Valuing righteousness over unjust gain.
- **Proverbs 10:9**: Walking securely with integrity.

End of Chapter 8

CHAPTER 9: CULTIVATING A STRONG WORK ETHIC

"And whatever you do, do it heartily, as to the Lord and not to men." — *Colossians 3:23*

Introduction

A strong work ethic is a fundamental component of personal fulfillment and organizational success. The Bible consistently promotes virtues like diligence, dedication, and excellence in one's endeavors. *Colossians 3:23* encourages us to approach our work with enthusiasm and sincerity, viewing it as service to the Lord rather than merely to human masters. This perspective elevates the significance of our daily tasks and inspires a higher level of commitment. This chapter explores how cultivating a strong work ethic benefits both individuals and organizations, delving into motivating employees beyond monetary incentives, the role of passion in work, and balancing hard work with rest.

Motivating Employees Beyond Monetary Incentives

Understanding Intrinsic Vs. Extrinsic Motivation

- **Extrinsic Motivation**: Driven by external rewards such as money, promotions, or recognition.
- **Intrinsic Motivation**: Driven by internal rewards like personal growth, fulfillment, and a sense of purpose.

Biblical Foundation

- **Service with Sincerity**

  - **"Not with eye-service, as men-pleasers, but as bondservants of Christ, doing the will of God from the heart."** — *Ephesians 6:6*

   This verse emphasizes working earnestly, not just when being watched or for external approval, but with genuine commitment.

Strategies To Enhance Intrinsic Motivation

1. **Provide Meaningful Work**

   - **Align Tasks with Purpose**

- **Mission Connection**: Help employees understand how their roles contribute to the organization's mission and impact society positively.
   - **Autonomy**: Allow employees to have a degree of control over how they complete their tasks, fostering a sense of ownership.

2. **Foster a Positive Work Environment**

   - **Supportive Culture**

      - **Collaboration**: Encourage teamwork and open communication.
      - **Recognition**: Acknowledge achievements and efforts, reinforcing that their contributions are valued.

3. **Opportunities for Growth**

   - **Professional Development**

      - **Training Programs**: Offer workshops, courses, and mentoring to enhance skills.
      - **Career Advancement**: Provide clear pathways for progression within the organization.

4. **Encourage Creativity and Innovation**

   - **Idea Generation**

      - **Brainstorming Sessions**: Involve employees in problem-solving and decision-making processes.
      - **Reward Innovation**: Recognize and implement valuable employee suggestions.

Benefits Of Intrinsic Motivation

- **Increased Engagement**: Employees are more invested in their work.
- **Higher Productivity**: Intrinsically motivated individuals often exceed performance expectations.
- **Reduced Turnover**: Satisfaction with work reduces the likelihood of employees seeking opportunities elsewhere.

Biblical Insight

- ***"The soul of the sluggard craves and gets nothing, while the soul of the diligent is richly supplied."*** — *Proverbs 13:4*

Diligence leads to fulfillment and abundance, not just materially but also in personal satisfaction.

The Role of Passion in Work

Defining Passion In The Workplace

- **Passion**: A strong inclination toward an activity that individuals like, find important, and in which they invest time and energy.

Biblical Foundation

- **Wholehearted Commitment**

 - ***"Whatever your hand finds to do, do it with your might."*** — *Ecclesiastes 9:10*

 This encourages giving one's best effort in all endeavors.

Cultivating Passion Among Employees

1. **Align Roles with Strengths and Interests**

 - **Skill Assessment**

 - **Personal Strengths**: Identify employees' talents and assign tasks that leverage these abilities.
 - **Interest Surveys**: Understand what aspects of work employees are most passionate about.

2. **Set Challenging Yet Achievable Goals**

 - **Goal Setting**

 - **SMART Goals**: Specific, Measurable, Achievable, Relevant, Time-bound.
 - **Progress Tracking**: Regularly review goals to maintain motivation and adjust as necessary.

3. **Create a Vision for the Future**

 - **Career Pathing**

 - **Long-Term Opportunities**: Discuss future possibilities and help employees envision their growth.
 - **Mentorship**: Pair employees with mentors who inspire and

guide them.

4. **Encourage Ownership**

  - **Empowerment**

    - **Decision-Making**: Allow employees to make decisions related to their work.
    - **Accountability**: Encourage taking responsibility for outcomes, fostering a deeper connection to the work.

Impact Of Passionate Employees

- **Enhanced Creativity**: Passion fuels innovation and problem-solving.
- **Resilience**: Passionate individuals are more likely to persevere through challenges.
- **Positive Workplace Culture**: Enthusiasm is contagious, boosting overall morale.

Biblical Insight

- **"Delight yourself in the LORD, and he will give you the desires of your heart."** — *Psalm 37:4*

  Finding joy and purpose in one's work aligns with receiving fulfillment and satisfaction.

Balancing Hard Work with Rest

-**The Necessity of Rest**
- **Preventing Burnout**: Continuous work without rest leads to physical and mental exhaustion.
- **Enhancing Productivity**: Rest rejuvenates the mind and body, improving focus and efficiency.

Biblical Foundation

- **Sabbath Principle**

  - **"Six days you shall labor and do all your work, but the seventh day is the Sabbath of the LORD your God. In it you shall do no work."** — *Exodus 20:9-10*

  This commandment emphasizes the importance of rest as part of the work cycle.

Implementing Work-Rest Balance

1. **Promote a Culture that Values Rest**

   - **Lead by Example**

     - **Leadership Practices**: Leaders should model healthy work-rest habits.
     - **Encourage Time Off**: Actively support employees in taking vacations and breaks.

2. **Establish Reasonable Work Hours**

- **Workload Management**

    - **Prevent Overwork**: Monitor workloads to ensure they are manageable.
    - **Flexible Scheduling**: Offer flexible hours or remote work options when possible.

3. **Provide Rest Spaces**

   - **Physical Environment**

     - **Break Areas**: Create comfortable spaces for employees to relax during breaks.
     - **Wellness Programs**: Offer activities that promote relaxation and stress reduction.

4. **Educate on the Importance of Rest**

   - **Workshops and Seminars**

     - **Health Benefits**: Share information on how rest improves health and performance.
     - **Productivity Gains**: Highlight how rest leads to better work outcomes.

Benefits Of Balanced Work And Rest

- **Improved Health**: Reduces stress-related illnesses and enhances well-being.
- **Increased Efficiency**: Rested employees are more alert and productive.
- **Employee Satisfaction**: Promotes a supportive work environment, boosting morale.

Biblical Insight

- **"It is in vain that you rise up early and go late to rest, eating the bread of anxious toil; for he gives to his beloved sleep."** — *Psalm 127:2*

Overworking without rest is ultimately unproductive; rest is a gift that should be embraced.

Practical Steps to Cultivate a Strong Work Ethic

1. Define and Communicate Expectations

  - **Clear Guidelines**

    - **Work Standards**: Establish what constitutes quality work and expected behaviors.
    - **Performance Metrics**: Use objective measures to evaluate work ethic.

2. Provide Training and Development

  - **Skill Enhancement**

    - **Workshops**: Offer sessions on time management, goal setting, and productivity.
    - **Mentoring**: Pair employees with mentors who exemplify a strong work ethic.

3. Recognize and Reward Diligence

- **Acknowledgment**

   - **Verbal Praise**: Regularly acknowledge hard work and dedication.
   - **Incentives**: Offer bonuses, promotions, or other rewards for exemplary work.

4. Foster a Supportive Environment

- **Team Building**

   - **Collaboration**: Encourage teamwork and mutual support.
   - **Open Communication**: Create an environment where employees feel comfortable sharing ideas and concerns.

5. Lead by Example

- **Demonstrate Commitment**

   - **Work Ethic**: Leaders should model the dedication and diligence they wish to see.
   - **Ethical Behavior**: Uphold integrity and honesty in all actions.

Conclusion

Cultivating a strong work ethic is vital for both personal fulfillment and organizational success. By motivating employees beyond monetary incentives, fostering passion in their work, and balancing hard work with necessary rest, businesses can create an environment where individuals thrive, and collective goals are achieved. The biblical principles highlight that work is not merely a means to an end but an opportunity to serve with excellence and dedication. Embracing these values leads to a more engaged workforce, higher productivity, and a positive organizational culture that benefits everyone involved.

Reflection Questions

1. **Intrinsic Motivation**: How can your organization enhance intrinsic motivation among employees?

2. **Passion and Purpose**: In what ways can you help employees find passion and purpose in their work?

3. **Work-Rest Balance**: What strategies can you implement to ensure employees balance hard work with adequate rest?

Key Scriptures for Further Reflection

- **Colossians 3:23**: Working heartily as unto the Lord.
- **Proverbs 13:4**: The soul of the diligent is richly supplied.
- **Ecclesiastes 9:10**: Doing whatever your hand finds to do with all your might.
- **Psalm 127:2**: The importance of rest as a gift from God.
- **Ephesians 6:6**: Serving sincerely from the heart.

- **Proverbs 22:29**: A diligent person will stand before kings.

End of Chapter 9

CHAPTER 10: NAVIGATING COMPETITION AND CONFLICT

"But I say to you, love your enemies and pray for those who persecute you." — *Matthew 5:44*

Introduction

In the dynamic world of business, competition and conflict are inevitable. While competition can drive innovation and improvement, it can also lead to unethical behaviors if not managed properly. Conflicts may arise not only with competitors but also within organizations and among stakeholders. The Bible offers profound wisdom on handling adversaries and conflicts with grace, integrity, and strategic wisdom. *Matthew 5:44* challenges us to "love your enemies and pray for those who persecute you," urging a paradigm shift in how we perceive and interact with those we might consider opponents. This chapter explores ethical competition strategies, conflict resolution and reconciliation, and the potential for collaborating with competitors for mutual benefit.

Ethical Competition Strategies

Understanding Ethical Competition

Ethical competition involves striving to achieve business success without compromising moral principles or engaging in unfair practices. It emphasizes integrity, fairness, and respect for competitors, customers, and the broader community.

Biblical Foundation

- **Honoring Integrity**
- **"Better is a poor man who walks in his integrity than a rich man who is crooked in his ways."** — *Proverbs 28:6*

This verse highlights the value of integrity over ill-gotten gains, emphasizing that ethical conduct is more important than wealth acquired through unethical means.

Principles Of Ethical Competition

1. **Transparency**

  - **Honest Marketing**

    - Avoid misleading advertisements and exaggerations.

- Clearly communicate product features, benefits, and limitations.

  - **Open Communication**

    - Be forthright with stakeholders about company practices and policies.

2. **Fair Pricing**

  - **Competitive but Just**

    - Set prices that reflect the value provided without engaging in predatory pricing to undermine competitors unjustly.

3. **Respect for Competitors**

  - **Professional Conduct**

    - Refrain from disparaging competitors.
    - Focus on highlighting your own strengths rather than exploiting competitors' weaknesses.

4. **Compliance with Laws and Regulations**

  - **Legal Adherence**

    - Abide by all applicable laws, including antitrust laws, consumer protection regulations, and industry standards.

5. **Innovation and Improvement**

  - **Value Addition**

    - Invest in research and development to improve products and services genuinely.

- Encourage creativity within the organization to stay ahead ethically.

Application in Business

- **Ethical Marketing Campaigns**

  - Develop campaigns that truthfully represent offerings and respect the intelligence of consumers.

- **Corporate Policies**

  - Establish codes of conduct that define acceptable competitive behaviors and enforce them consistently.

  - **Employee Training**

  - Educate employees on ethical standards and the importance of integrity in competitive practices.

Benefits Of Ethical Competition

- **Customer Trust**

  - Builds a loyal customer base that values honesty and integrity.

- **Reputation Enhancement**

  - Establishes the company as a respectable player in the industry.

- **Sustainable Success**

  - Promotes long-term growth by avoiding legal issues and

maintaining positive relationships.

Biblical Insight

- *"Do to others as you would have them do to you."* — *Luke 6:31*

This "Golden Rule" encourages treating competitors with the same respect and fairness one would expect in return.

Conflict Resolution and Reconciliation

Understanding Conflict In Business

Conflicts can occur internally among employees, between management and staff, or externally with customers, suppliers, and competitors. Effective conflict resolution is essential to maintain healthy relationships and organizational harmony.

Biblical Foundation

- **Pursuing Peace**

 - *"If it is possible, as far as it depends on you, live at peace with everyone."* — *Romans 12:18*

This verse urges individuals to strive for peace in all relationships, taking responsibility for their part in resolving conflicts.

Steps For Effective Conflict Resolution

1. **Acknowledge the Conflict**

   - **Open Recognition**

     - Identify and admit that a conflict exists.
     - Encourage a culture where issues can be raised without fear.

2. **Seek Understanding**

   - **Active Listening**

     - Listen to all parties involved to understand their perspectives.
     - Avoid interrupting or dismissing concerns.

3. **Communicate Respectfully**

   - **Constructive Dialogue**

     - Use respectful language.
     - Focus on the issue at hand, not personal attacks.

4. **Identify Common Ground**

   - **Shared Goals**

     - Find areas of agreement that can serve as a foundation for resolution.

- Emphasize mutual interests over differences.

5. **Collaborate on Solutions**

   - **Joint Problem-Solving**

     - Involve all parties in generating possible solutions.
     - Evaluate options based on fairness and mutual benefit.

6. **Agree on a Resolution**

   - **Commitment**

     - Reach a consensus on the best course of action.
     - Document agreements to ensure clarity.

7. **Follow Up**

   - **Ensure Implementation**

     - Monitor the situation to ensure the resolution is effective.
     - Be open to making adjustments if necessary.

Application In Business

- **Mediation and Facilitation**

   - Use neutral third parties to facilitate discussions when conflicts are particularly challenging.

- **Conflict Resolution Training**

   - Provide employees and managers with training on effective communication and conflict management techniques.

- **Policies and Procedures**

   - Establish clear guidelines for addressing conflicts, including reporting mechanisms and escalation paths.

Reconciliation

- **Forgiveness and Restoration**

   - Encourage a culture where forgiveness is valued, and relationships can be restored after conflicts.

- **Biblical Example**

   - **Joseph and His Brothers**: Joseph forgave his brothers who sold him into slavery, leading to family reconciliation (*Genesis 50:15-21*).

Biblical Insight

- **"Blessed are the peacemakers, for they will be called children of God."** — *Matthew 5:9*

   Peacemakers play a crucial role in fostering harmony and are commended for their efforts.

Collaborating with Competitors for Mutual Benefit

Understanding Coopetition

- **Coopetition**: A blend of cooperation and competition where companies work together on shared goals while still remaining competitors in other areas.

Biblical Foundation

- **Unity and Collaboration**

  - **"Two are better than one, because they have a good return for their labor."** — *Ecclesiastes 4:9*

    This verse emphasizes the benefits of collaboration and collective effort.

Benefits Of Collaborating With Competitors

1. **Resource Sharing**

   - **Cost Reduction**

     - Share costs for research, development, or infrastructure.

   - **Expertise Exchange**

     - Combine knowledge and skills for mutual advancement.

2. **Market Expansion**

   - **Joint Ventures**

- Enter new markets together to share risks and benefits.

  - **Standardization**

    - Develop industry standards that benefit all parties.

3. **Innovation Acceleration**

   - **Collaborative Innovation**

     - Pool resources to innovate faster than working individually.

4. **Addressing Common Challenges**

   - **Industry Issues**

     - Work together on regulatory compliance, sustainability, or ethical sourcing.

Strategies for Effective Collaboration

1. **Identify Common Goals**

   - **Mutual Interests**

     - Find areas where collaboration is beneficial to all parties involved.

2. **Establish Clear Agreements**

   - **Contracts and MOUs**

     - Formalize the terms of collaboration to prevent misunderstandings.

3. **Maintain Open Communication**

- **Regular Meetings**

    - Keep all parties informed and engaged throughout the collaboration.

4. **Respect Confidentiality**

    - **Information Security**

        - Protect sensitive information and honor confidentiality agreements.

5. **Monitor and Evaluate**

    - **Performance Metrics**

        - Set benchmarks to assess the effectiveness of the collaboration.

Examples Of Successful Collaboration

- **Joint Research Projects**

    - Companies in the pharmaceutical industry often collaborate on research to develop new drugs.

- **Industry Consortia**

    - Technology firms may form alliances to establish common standards (e.g., USB standards).

Biblical Insight

- **"As iron sharpens iron, so one person sharpens another."** — *Proverbs 27:17*

Collaborating can enhance capabilities and lead to mutual improvement.

Applying Biblical Principles to Competition and Conflict

Loving Your Enemies

- **Radical Approach**

  - **"But I say to you, love your enemies and pray for those who persecute you."** — *Matthew 5:44*

This teaching encourages showing kindness and goodwill even towards adversaries.

Practical Applications

1. **Respectful Conduct**

   - **Professionalism**

- Treat competitors and adversaries with respect, regardless of their actions.

2. **Avoid Retaliation**

   - **Grace Over Vengeance**

   - Do not engage in vindictive behaviors when wronged.

3. **Seek to Understand**

   - **Empathy**

   - Try to understand the perspectives and motivations of competitors and adversaries.

4. **Pray and Reflect**

   - **Spiritual Practice**

   - Pray for wisdom in handling conflicts and for the well-being of those involved.

Benefits Of This Approach

- **Personal Peace**

   - Reduces stress and resentment, leading to better decision-making.

- **Positive Reputation**

   - Demonstrates integrity and ethical leadership.

- **Opportunities for Reconciliation**

   - Opens doors for resolving conflicts and building stronger relationships.

Case Studies of Ethical Competition and Conflict Resolution

Case Study 1: The Cola Wars

- **Background**

   - Coca-Cola and PepsiCo have been fierce competitors for decades.

- **Ethical Breach**

   - In 2006, PepsiCo alerted Coca-Cola that some of Coca-Cola's confidential information was being offered to PepsiCo by a Coca-Cola employee.

- **Outcome**

   - PepsiCo's ethical decision to inform Coca-Cola led to the arrest of the individuals involved.

- **Lesson**

   - Upholding ethical standards strengthens industry integrity and fosters mutual respect.

Case Study 2: Apple and Samsung

- **Background**

  - Both companies compete in the smartphone market but have collaborated in other areas.

- **Collaboration**

  - Samsung supplies components for Apple's devices.

- **Conflict**

  - Legal battles over patent infringements.

- **Lesson**

  - Companies can navigate competition and conflict by compartmentalizing collaboration and competition, maintaining professional relationships despite disputes.

Practical Steps for Navigating Competition and Conflict

1. Develop an Ethical Framework

  - **Policies and Guidelines**

  - Create a code of ethics that outlines acceptable competitive behaviors.

  - **Training**

- Educate employees on ethical standards and conflict resolution techniques.

2. Foster a Culture of Respect

  - **Leadership Example**

    - Leaders should model respectful behavior towards competitors and in conflicts.

  - **Employee Engagement**

    - Encourage employees to voice concerns and ideas respectfully.

3. Implement Conflict Resolution Mechanisms

  - **Mediation Processes**

    - Establish procedures for addressing internal and external conflicts.

  - **Feedback Systems**

    - Create channels for stakeholders to express grievances constructively.

4. Explore Collaborative Opportunities

  - **Identify Potential Partnerships**

    - Look for areas where working with competitors could be mutually beneficial.

  - **Build Trust**

- Start with small projects to build confidence in collaborative relationships.

5. Embrace Forgiveness and Reconciliation

- **Address Past Conflicts**

  - Seek to resolve lingering disputes that may hinder progress.

- **Focus on the Future**

  - Prioritize long-term relationships over short-term gains.

Conclusion

Navigating competition and conflict with grace, integrity, and strategic wisdom is not only possible but also beneficial for long-term success. By embracing ethical competition strategies, effectively resolving conflicts, and exploring collaborative opportunities with competitors, businesses can operate in a manner that aligns with biblical principles. *Matthew 5:44* challenges us to rise above adversarial instincts and approach competition and conflict with love and compassion. Implementing these principles leads to a more ethical, respectful, and ultimately prosperous business environment.

Reflection Questions

1. **Ethical Competition**: How can your organization ensure that its competitive strategies are ethical and respectful?

2. **Conflict Resolution**: What mechanisms are in place to address conflicts within your organization? How can they be improved?

3. **Collaboration Opportunities**: Are there areas where collaborating with competitors could be mutually beneficial? How might you pursue these opportunities?

Key Scriptures for Further Reflection

- **Matthew 5:44**: Loving enemies and praying for persecutors.
- **Proverbs 28:6**: Integrity over ill-gotten wealth.
- **Romans 12:18**: Living at peace with everyone.
- **Luke 6:31**: Treating others as you would like to be treated.
- **Matthew 5:9**: Blessings for peacemakers.
- **Proverbs 27:17**: Mutual improvement through collaboration.
- **Ecclesiastes 4:9**: The benefits of working together.

End of Chapter 10

CHAPTER 11: THE PRINCIPLE OF REST AND RENEWAL

"Remember the Sabbath day, to keep it holy." — *Exodus 20:8*

ntroduction

In the relentless pace of modern business, the value of rest is often underestimated or overlooked. The pursuit of success and productivity can lead to a culture where overwork is normalized, and rest is perceived as a luxury rather than a necessity. However, the Bible emphasizes the importance of rest as a divine principle, starting from the creation narrative where God rested on the seventh day. *Exodus 20:8* commands us to "Remember the Sabbath day, to keep it holy," highlighting rest not just as a physical need but as a sacred practice. This chapter explores how incorporating rest and renewal into our lives and workplaces enhances productivity, fosters creativity, and contributes to overall well-being. By understanding the significance of work-life balance, we can create environments that promote sustained success and job satisfaction.

Preventing Burnout in the Workplace

Understanding Burnout

Burnout is a state of physical, emotional, and mental exhaustion caused by prolonged stress and overwork. It can lead to decreased productivity, health issues, and a diminished quality of life.

Biblical Foundation

- **Limits of Human Capacity**
- **"It is in vain that you rise up early and go late to rest, eating the bread of anxious toil; for He gives to His beloved sleep."** — *Psalm 127:2*

This verse emphasizes that relentless labor without rest is ultimately unproductive and that rest is a gift from God.

Causes Of Burnout

1. **Excessive Workload**

   - **Unrealistic Expectations**: Constant high demands without sufficient resources or time.

2. **Lack of Control**

- **Autonomy**: Feeling powerless over one's work can increase stress levels.

3. **Insufficient Rewards**

   - **Recognition**: Lack of appreciation or adequate compensation can lead to disengagement.

4. **Poor Workplace Relationships**

   - **Isolation**: Limited support from colleagues or supervisors exacerbates stress.

5. **Work-Life Imbalance**

   - **Neglect of Personal Life**: Overemphasis on work at the expense of personal and family time.

Strategies to Prevent Burnout

1. **Promote a Culture of Rest**

   - **Leadership Example**: Leaders should model balanced work habits, taking breaks and vacations.
   - **Policy Implementation**: Establish guidelines that encourage reasonable work hours and discourage excessive overtime.

2. **Workload Management**

   - **Resource Allocation**: Ensure adequate staffing and distribute tasks evenly.
   - **Priority Setting**: Help employees focus on high-impact activities.

3. **Enhance Employee Autonomy**

   - **Empowerment**: Allow employees to have a say in how they accomplish their tasks.
   - **Flexibility**: Offer options like flexible schedules or remote work when possible.

4. **Recognition and Rewards**

   - **Appreciation Programs**: Regularly acknowledge and reward contributions.
   - **Feedback Mechanisms**: Provide constructive feedback and opportunities for growth.

5. **Foster Supportive Relationships**

   - **Team Building**: Encourage collaboration and camaraderie among team members.
   - **Open Communication**: Create an environment where employees feel comfortable sharing concerns.

6. **Promote Work-Life Balance**

   - **Boundaries**: Encourage employees to disconnect after work hours.
   - **Wellness Programs**: Offer resources for physical and mental health.

Biblical Insight

- **Jesus' Example of Rest**

  - *"Then, because so many people were coming and going that they did not even have a chance to eat, He said to them, 'Come with Me by yourselves to a quiet place and get some rest."** — *Mark 6:31*

Even in the midst of demanding ministry, Jesus recognized the need for rest and encouraged His disciples to take time away.

Encouraging Employees to Take Time Off

Understanding The Reluctance To Rest

- **Cultural Pressures**: Fear of appearing less dedicated or missing out on opportunities.
- **Workload Concerns**: Anxiety about falling behind or burdening colleagues.

Biblical Foundation

- **Sabbath Rest as a Command**

  - *"Six days you shall labor and do all your work, but the seventh day is a Sabbath to the LORD your God. On it you shall not do any work..."** — *Exodus 20:9-10*

The commandment emphasizes rest as an integral part of the work cycle, mandated by God.

Strategies to Encourage Time Off

1. **Establish Clear Policies**

   - **Paid Time Off (PTO)**: Provide adequate vacation days and personal leave.
   - **Mandatory Breaks**: Implement policies requiring employees to take minimum time off annually.

2. **Normalize Taking Leave**

   - **Leadership Participation**: When leaders take vacations, it sets a precedent.
   - **Success Stories**: Share positive outcomes of employees returning refreshed after time off.

3. **Streamline Work Processes**

   - **Cross-Training**: Ensure others can cover responsibilities during absences.
   - **Workload Planning**: Adjust deadlines and expectations around planned leaves.

4. **Communicate Benefits**

   - **Health and Productivity**: Educate employees on how rest improves performance and well-being.
   - **Preventative Approach**: Emphasize rest as a means to prevent burnout and long-term absenteeism.

5. **Recognize Rest as Part of Performance**

   - **Incorporate into Evaluations**: Acknowledge effective time management, including appropriate use of leave.
   - **Reward Balance**: Encourage and recognize employees who maintain a healthy work-life balance.

Biblical Insight

- **Rest Leads to Renewal**

  - **"He makes me lie down in green pastures, He leads me beside quiet waters, He restores my soul."** — *Psalm 23:2-3*

  Rest is depicted as restorative, nourishing both the soul and the body.

The Benefits of Rest on Decision-Making and Leadership

Rest Enhances Cognitive Functions

- **Improved Concentration**: Rest reduces fatigue, improving focus.
- **Better Memory**: Sleep and relaxation aid in memory consolidation.
- **Enhanced Creativity**: Restful periods allow the mind to process information subconsciously, leading to insights.

Biblical Foundation

- **Wisdom in Rest**

  - **"In vain you rise early and stay up late, toiling for food to eat

—for He grants sleep to those He loves."** — *Psalm 127:2*

Acknowledges that overexertion is futile and that God provides rest as a blessing.

Impact On Leadership

1. **Clarity in Decision-Making**

   - **Reduced Stress**: Rested leaders are less likely to make decisions based on stress or emotion.
   - **Perspective**: Time away can provide new viewpoints on challenges.

2. **Emotional Intelligence**

   - **Patience and Empathy**: Rested individuals are better equipped to handle interpersonal relations.
   - **Conflict Resolution**: Calmness derived from rest aids in resolving disputes effectively.

3. **Modeling Healthy Behavior**

   - **Influence**: Leaders who prioritize rest set a standard for their teams.
   - **Credibility**: Demonstrates commitment to overall well-being, not just productivity.

Strategies for Leaders

1. **Schedule Regular Rest**

   - **Personal Time Off**: Plan vacations and breaks in advance.
   - **Daily Routines**: Incorporate rest periods into the daily

schedule.

2. **Mindfulness and Reflection**

   - **Quiet Time**: Dedicate time for meditation, prayer, or reflection.
   - **Journaling**: Record thoughts and experiences to process emotions and ideas.

3. **Delegate Responsibilities**

   - **Empower Team Members**: Trust others to handle tasks, reducing personal workload.
   - **Succession Planning**: Prepare others to step in when needed.

4. **Avoid Decision Fatigue**

   - **Prioritize Decisions**: Focus on high-impact decisions when rested.
   - **Limit Choices**: Streamline options to reduce mental overload.

Biblical Insight

- **Jesus Taking Time to Rest and Pray**

   - **"But Jesus often withdrew to lonely places and prayed."** — *Luke 5:16*

   Even with pressing demands, Jesus took time to withdraw and renew, setting an example for leadership.

Practical Steps to Implement Rest and Renewal in the Workplace

1. Develop Organizational Policies Supporting Rest

  - **Rest-Friendly Policies**

    - **Mandatory Breaks**: Enforce lunch breaks and short breaks during the workday.
    - **No After-Hours Communication**: Limit emails and calls outside of work hours.

  - **Flexible Work Arrangements**

    - **Remote Work Options**: Provide flexibility to work from home when appropriate.
    - **Flexible Scheduling**: Allow for varied work hours to accommodate personal needs.

2. Create a Rest-Conducive Environment

  - **Rest Spaces**

    - **Quiet Rooms**: Designate areas for relaxation or meditation.
    - **Ergonomic Workstations**: Invest in comfortable furniture and equipment.

  - **Wellness Programs**

    - **Physical Health**: Offer fitness classes, gym memberships, or health screenings.
    - **Mental Health**: Provide access to counseling services or

stress management resources.

3. Educate and Promote Awareness

  - **Workshops and Seminars**

    - Stress Management: Teach techniques for coping with stress.
    - Time Management: Help employees prioritize tasks to prevent overwork.

  - **Communication Campaigns**

    - Regular Reminders: Share articles or tips on the importance of rest.
    - Success Stories: Highlight examples of improved performance due to rest.

4. Monitor and Adjust Workloads

  - Regular Check-Ins

    - One-on-One Meetings: Discuss workload and stress levels with employees.
    - Team Assessments: Evaluate team capacity and redistribute tasks as needed.

  - Avoid Over-Scheduling

    - Realistic Deadlines* Set achievable timelines for projects.
    - Resource Planning: Ensure teams have the necessary support to meet demands.

5. Encourage a Culture of Trust

  - **Open Dialogue**

- Feedback Channels: Create safe spaces for employees to express concerns.
  - Transparency: Be honest about organizational challenges and efforts to address them.

  - Lead by Example
    - Leadership Participation: When leaders prioritize rest, it legitimizes the practice.
    - Acknowledgment: Recognize and appreciate employees who maintain balance.

Conclusion

The principle of rest and renewal is not merely a personal luxury but a vital component of organizational health and effectiveness. By embracing rest as an integral part of the work cycle, businesses can prevent burnout, enhance decision-making, and foster a more engaged and satisfied workforce. The biblical command to "Remember the Sabbath day, to keep it holy" serves as a reminder that rest is both a divine ordinance and a practical necessity. Integrating rest into the corporate culture promotes sustainable productivity, sparks creativity, and ultimately contributes to the flourishing of both individuals and organizations.

Reflection Questions

1. Assessing Workload: Are employees in your organization experiencing signs of burnout? What steps can be taken to alleviate this?

2. Promoting Rest: How does your company currently encourage employees to take time off? What improvements can be made?

3. Leadership Practices: As a leader, how do you model the importance of rest and renewal to your team?

Key Scriptures for Further Reflection

- Exodus 20:8-10: The commandment to observe the Sabbath.
- Psalm 127:2: The futility of overwork and the gift of rest.
- Mark 6:31: Jesus invites His disciples to rest.
- Psalm 23:2-3: Rest as restoration of the soul.
- Luke 5:16: Jesus often withdrew to pray and rest.
- Ecclesiastes 3:1: "There is a time for everything..."

End of Chapter 11

CHAPTER 12: CONCLUSION: BUILDING A BUSINESS THAT LASTS

Applying biblical principles to business is more than a moral directive; it's a transformative approach that builds organizations capable of enduring challenges and making a lasting impact. Throughout this book, we've explored how timeless wisdom from the Bible can guide modern leaders in creating businesses that are not only successful but also ethical, sustainable, and socially responsible.

The Foundation Of Integrity And Honesty

In **Chapter 1**, we discussed how integrity and honesty form the bedrock of trust in any business relationship. Upholding these values cultivates a reputation that attracts customers, retains employees, and fosters partnerships. In a world where shortcuts and unethical practices may offer temporary gains, a commitment to integrity ensures long-term success and stability.

Stewardship And Responsible Management

Chapter 2 highlighted the importance of stewardship and the wise management of resources. By viewing assets—whether financial, human, or environmental—as entrusted to us, we recognize our responsibility to manage them wisely. This approach leads to sustainable growth and positions businesses as conscientious contributors to society.

Leadership Guided By Wisdom

Drawing from **Chapter 3** and **Chapter 4**, we examined leadership lessons from biblical figures like Moses, Nehemiah, and King Solomon. Their examples teach us the value of seeking wisdom, embracing humility, and making decisions that benefit the greater good. Leaders who prioritize wisdom over personal ambition inspire trust and guide their organizations toward meaningful achievements.

The Transformative Power Of Servant Leadership

In **Chapter 5**, we explored servant leadership as a model that turns traditional hierarchies upside down. By serving employees and customers, leaders foster an environment of empowerment, collaboration, and innovation. This approach not only enhances organizational culture but also drives performance and loyalty.

Balancing Wealth With Ethical Responsibility

Chapter 6 addressed the pursuit of profit within the bounds of ethical considerations. Wealth should be viewed as a tool for good, not an end in itself. Businesses that balance profit-making with philanthropy and social responsibility contribute positively to society while avoiding the pitfalls of greed.

Justice, Fairness, And Ethical Practices

In **Chapter 7**, we emphasized the necessity of justice and fairness in all business dealings. Fair labor practices, equitable treatment of customers, and advocacy for just industry regulations build trust and strengthen relationships with all stakeholders. These principles are essential for creating a just economy and a reputable brand.

The Importance Of Vision And Strategic Planning

Chapter 8 underscored the role of a clear vision and strategic planning in guiding a company's direction. Aligning goals with ethical values ensures that decisions contribute to long-term success and uphold the organization's mission. A well-crafted vision inspires stakeholders and provides a roadmap for sustainable growth.

Cultivating A Strong Work Ethic While Embracing Rest

In **Chapter 9** and **Chapter 11**, we delved into the significance of diligence balanced with rest. Encouraging a strong work ethic enhances productivity and fulfillment, but recognizing the need for rest prevents burnout and fosters creativity. A balanced approach leads to sustained performance and employee well-being.

Navigating Competition And Conflict With Integrity

Chapter 10 explored strategies for handling competition and conflicts ethically. By approaching these challenges with grace, integrity, and strategic wisdom, businesses can maintain positive relationships and uphold their reputations. Ethical competition fosters innovation and elevates industry standards.

Building A Legacy Of Impact

By integrating these biblical principles, businesses can build legacies that extend beyond financial success. They become agents of positive change, influencing industries and communities for the better. Such organizations not only endure but also inspire others to adopt values that promote the common good.

A Call To Action

As we conclude this exploration of biblical principles in business, the invitation is clear: embrace these timeless values in your leadership and organizational practices. Whether you're a seasoned executive or an aspiring entrepreneur, integrating integrity, stewardship, servant leadership, and ethical decision-making into your business will yield dividends that surpass monetary gains.

CHAPTER 13: FINAL THOUGHTS

As we reach the culmination of this exploration into the intersection of biblical principles and modern business practices, it's essential to pause and reflect on the journey we've undertaken. The chapters preceding this one have delved into the timeless wisdom of the Bible, uncovering insights that are as relevant today as they were thousands of years ago. These principles are not confined to religious contexts; they offer practical guidance for anyone seeking to build a business that is resilient, ethical, and impactful.

Embracing Timeless Wisdom In A Modern World

The challenges of today's business environment are complex and multifaceted. Globalization, technological innovation, and rapidly changing market dynamics demand agility and foresight. Amidst this whirlwind of change, biblical principles provide a steady compass. They ground us in values that transcend profit margins and market shares, reminding us of the greater purpose behind our endeavors.

- Integrity and Honesty: In a world where misinformation can spread rapidly, maintaining integrity builds trust and credibility.
- Stewardship and Responsibility: Responsible management of resources ensures sustainability and long-term success.
- Wisdom and Discernment: Making informed decisions requires not just data but also wisdom and ethical consideration.
- Servant Leadership: Prioritizing the well-being of others fosters a positive organizational culture and drives collective success.

The Human Element In Business

At the heart of every business are people—employees, customers, partners, and communities. Recognizing this human element transforms how we approach leadership and management. It's not merely about transactions but about relationships built on respect, empathy, and mutual benefit.

- Empowering Employees: By investing in the growth and well-

being of our teams, we unlock their full potential.
- Serving Customers: Understanding and meeting the genuine needs of customers creates lasting loyalty.
- Engaging with Communities: Businesses have the power to effect positive change in the communities they serve.

Balancing Profit With Purpose

Financial success and ethical responsibility are not mutually exclusive. In fact, they often reinforce each other. Companies that align their operations with ethical principles tend to enjoy enhanced reputations, customer loyalty, and employee satisfaction—all of which contribute to profitability.

- Ethical Profit-Making: Pursuing profit should never come at the expense of ethical standards.
- Philanthropy and Giving Back: Generosity enriches both the giver and the receiver, creating a cycle of positive impact.
- Sustainable Practices: Environmental stewardship is not just a moral imperative but also a business necessity in an era of increasing ecological awareness.

Navigating Challenges With Grace

Conflicts, competition, and setbacks are inevitable in business. How we navigate these challenges defines our character and, by extension, the character of our organizations.

- Ethical Competition: Competing fairly and respectfully elevates the entire industry.
- Conflict Resolution: Addressing disputes with empathy and a willingness to understand leads to stronger relationships.

- Resilience in Adversity: A foundation built on solid principles provides strength during difficult times.

A Vision For The Future

Looking ahead, the integration of biblical principles into business is not merely about preserving traditions but about innovating for a better future. These principles encourage us to think beyond short-term gains and consider the long-term impact of our actions.

- Innovation Rooted in Values: Creativity flourishes in environments where ethical considerations guide exploration.
- Global Impact: In our interconnected world, businesses have the opportunity to make a positive difference on a global scale.
- Legacy Building: The true measure of success lies in the lasting contributions we make to society and the lives we touch.

Your Role In The Journey

As you close this book, consider the role you play in bringing these principles to life within your sphere of influence. Whether you're leading a multinational corporation, managing a small business, or contributing as part of a team, your actions matter.

- Personal Commitment: Embrace these values personally before expecting them from others.
- Influencing Others: Lead by example, inspiring those around

you to adopt ethical practices.
- Continuous Learning: Stay open to new insights and be willing to adapt as you grow.

An Invitation To Reflect And Act

The insights shared throughout this book are starting points for deeper reflection and action. I invite you to consider the following questions:

1. Self-Assessment: How do your personal values align with the way you conduct business?
2. Organizational Alignment: Are your company's policies and practices reflective of the principles discussed?
3. Community Engagement: In what ways can your business contribute more positively to society?
4. Future Goals: How can you incorporate these timeless principles into your strategic planning for sustainable success?

A Closing Thought

The journey of integrating biblical principles into business is continuous and ever-evolving. It's not about perfection but about commitment and progress. Each step taken towards ethical practice, servant leadership, and responsible stewardship brings us closer to building businesses that not only thrive economically but also enrich the world.

May you find wisdom, courage, and inspiration as you apply these principles in your professional journey. Remember that the impact of your efforts extends far beyond the balance sheet —it touches lives, shapes communities, and contributes to a legacy that endures.

Let us strive together to build businesses that last, not just in years but in the positive difference they make for generations to come.

www.ingramcontent.com/pod-product-compliance
Lightning Source LLC
Chambersburg PA
CBHW052318220526
45472CB00001B/172